Beat The Booze

A comprehensive guide to combating drink problems in
all walks of life

Reclaim your life

by

Edmund & Helen Tirbutt

HARRIMAN HOUSE LTD

3A Penns Road
Petersfield
Hampshire
GU32 2EW
GREAT BRITAIN

Tel: +44 (0)1730 233870
Fax: +44 (0)1730 233880
Email: enquiries@harriman-house.com
Website: www.harriman-house.com

First published in Great Britain in 2008
Copyright © Harriman House Ltd

The right of Edmund & Helen Tirbutt to be identified as authors has been asserted
in accordance with the Copyright, Design and Patents Acts 1988.

ISBN: 1-905641-42-7
ISBN 13: 978-1905641-42-0

British Library Cataloguing in Publication Data
A CIP catalogue record for this book can be obtained from the British Library.

Printed and bound by the CPI Group, William Clowes

Contents

Acknowledgements

We would like to put on record our immense gratitude to all the experts, case studies and other individuals and organisations who have helped us to produce this book.

About The Authors

Edmund Tirbutt

Edmund has been teetotal for over 21 years after drinking heavily during his years at university and subsequently finding it difficult to drink in moderation in his 20s. He tried various methods of cutting down and introduced rules to reduce his alcohol intake, including only drinking at weekends or when on holiday. Neither of these approaches  worked as he always ended up drinking to excess. His decision to quit was determined by the intervention of a friend – when he was 28 years old – who told him he would end up sad and alone and, most probably, soon dead if he did not quit the booze, which he then did almost immediately. Since then his life has changed beyond recognition. He fulfilled his ambition to become a journalist on the national papers, and during the final seven years of his journalistic career won a remarkable 18 awards for excellence.

Helen Tirbutt

Helen has been teetotal for over two years after deciding that life without alcohol is infinitely better than a life with it. She made the decision to quit drinking for lifestyle reasons. During her 20s and 30s, Helen worked in the City in the area of PR and Communications, and alcohol was very much a part of that lifestyle in the boom-bust years  throughout the 1980s and the 1990s. After setting up a copywriting company with her husband Edmund in 2004, she made many changes to her life, including moving out of London, taking up meditation and introducing healthier ways of dealing with work tension and stress. She quickly found that it is a total myth that you can't have a good time without alcohol, and realised that there are plenty of other healthier and more effective ways of dealing with the modern day worries that cause many people to drink.

Preface

Who this book is for

If you are concerned about your drinking, or about someone else's drinking, then this is the book for you. It is an easy to read, practical book with all the information you will need to help you cut down or cut out alcohol.

What the book covers

We consider virtually every conceivable method of combating alcohol consumption, ranging from conventional therapies to those that are less well known. Importantly, the book includes comprehensive contact details where you can get further help and information.

How the book is structured

The book is divided into two main sections. The first half focuses on how you can help yourself and the second half on how you can help others. The Appendices provide statistics, more detailed medical information and contact details.

Supporting website

A website supporting this book can be found at:

www.beatthebooze.com

Foreword

If you have picked up this book to help yourself or to help someone else, the chances are that you are looking for practical help and FAST.

"Beat The Booze" contains all the assistance we could find from interviewing leading experts in the field of alcohol addiction and individuals who have successfully cut down their drinking or given up alcohol altogether. Every chapter is packed with useful material about how to combat drink problems, and Appendix 3 contains contact details for a vast range of organisations that can provide you with professional help and further information.

The authors of this book have also been able to draw on extensive personal experience in battling alcohol, and our thoughts are with you as you walk this journey. Whether you have sunk to what you consider the greatest possible depths of despair or are merely seeking a healthier lifestyle, you can rest assured that we have also been there. So have the real-life case studies you will read about – some of whom have had their names or other personal details changed to preserve their anonymity. We have all emerged healthier, more productive and immeasurably happier.

Part 1

Helping Yourself

Chapter 1:
Forget The Word Alcoholic

It is time to forget the term 'alcoholic', which is one of the most outmoded and misleading words in the English language. Replace it with 'drink problem'.

If you're finding it difficult to exercise control over your levels of drinking, are suffering from regular hangovers or drinking when you are alone or feel down, then this book is for you.

You will find the government's safe drinking guidelines outlined at the end of this chapter, and other brief tests you can use to determine whether you have a drink problem are available in Appendix 1 (See pages 207 to 212). But the fact that you have picked up this book and started reading this section means that you probably already know the answer.

> "An alcoholic is a man you don't like who drinks as much as you do."
>
> Dylan Thomas

Most people with drink problems are capable of presenting a convincing case for why they are not an alcoholic, and regularly do so to their family and friends. For example, they can point out that they only ever drink in the evenings, that they never drink spirits, that they can give up for short periods, or that they can't remember the first time they drank alcohol – not because they're currently drunk but because they've heard that all alcoholics can!

Convenient shield

The term alcoholic can therefore act as a convenient shield for someone in denial about their drinking to hide behind. As long as they have not actually sunk to the level of that tramp they see swigging Tennents Extra every day near their local train station, they will take comfort from the fact that they do not consider themselves to be an alcoholic. This can make them suffer for longer than necessary as a result of failing to acknowledge and address their drink problem.

However mild someone's drink problem, their alcohol intake will gradually increase as their body becomes used to current levels and requires more to create the same effect. Delay therefore equals deterioration.

> **"If you're sick and tired of feeling sick and tired it's as good an indicator as any that you may have a drink problem."**
>
> Lucy Hogarth (See Case Study, Chapter 8, page 165)

From now onwards the word alcoholic will only appear in these pages when it forms part of an organisation's title or official creed.

The only statistic that matters is you

Furthermore, we have also confined medical gobbledegook and detailed statistics to our Appendices. We are acutely aware that boredom can actually exacerbate drink problems, and the only statistic we care about is you. Whatever percentage of others have succeeded or failed to beat the booze is of no relevance; you have it within you to triumph and overcome.

Whether we are throwing you a lifeline, offering you a lifestyle change, or both, the aim is to take you on an exciting journey that other individuals featured in this book have already been on.

Facing the music

If you had reason to believe that your car had developed a problem that could result in the engine blowing up while you were driving down the motorway, would you even think about not taking it into the garage to have it examined?

Similarly, if you were fairly sure that you had the first signs of a computer virus that could gradually corrupt all your data and eventually make your computer totally unusable, would you hesitate to call a computer engineer?

> "Alcohol is like the elephant in the sitting room that nobody talks about."
>
> Dr. Francis Keaney, Consultant Addiction Psychiatrist, National Addiction Centre, Institute of Psychiatry, King's College London

Don't delay

You may regularly try to convince yourself that you'll deal with the problem at some unspecified date in the future, but you always feel that you first need to negotiate some stressful hurdle in your life, such as an issue at work or a problem in a relationship or within your family. Try asking yourself how long you have been taking this attitude for and you are likely to conclude that the future should start now!

> 'If you were fairly sure that you had the first signs of a computer virus that could gradually corrupt all your data and eventually make your computer totally unusable, would you hesitate to call a computer engineer?'

Another common reason for delaying facing the music is fear of being told that you should never drink again, an idea that may seem totally unthinkable.

This will not necessarily happen. In Chapter 4 we demonstrate a number of strategies that have been used successfully by certain types of problem drinkers to reduce their alcohol intake. These have resulted in them leading happier and more fulfilled lives. There is, however, much to be said for going dry for at least an initial period whilst you are addressing the underlying issues that have been causing your drinking.

Nothing to fear

Even in cases where becoming completely teetotal is clearly the only solution, it doesn't mean that you will be endlessly craving alcohol or feeling that you will be losing out in any way. All you are giving up, apart from a series of temporary drug-induced highs, is a continuous source of problems, and in stopping you will command huge respect from those around you.

Indeed, you will actually become the envy of many. It may be hard to believe, but some teetotallers will tell you that if they have one major problem it is having to deal with jealousy from other people. Some may even try and sabotage your plans by encouraging you to drink.

Teetotallers often make ideal friends and partners because they never let out secrets when they are drunk, and they have more time to indulge in a wide range of interests. They also often excel in the workplace as a result of having more energy than most of their colleagues, and are less prone to taking time off and making errors (See Chapter 9).

> **"Work is the curse of the drinking classes."**
> Oscar Wilde

Time for a change

Many people who feel stuck in a rut are willing to consider making radical changes to their life to escape from the drudgery and routine that has been getting them down. They might, for example, risk changing careers in middle age or relocating to a foreign country. Why then should they not consider giving up drinking? It involves far less personal upheaval than emigrating to Australia and far less expense than retraining to become a lawyer! Indeed, giving up alcohol can enable you to realise significant financial savings and create considerable wealth. Not only will you no longer have to splash out on alcoholic drinks, you will also have a huge amount of new time available which can, if you wish, be used for earning money.

Who wants to be a millionaire?

Someone who defeats a serious drink problem and uses only half the time that becomes available through their new found sobriety could become wealthy beyond their wildest dreams.

Even if they never drank at lunchtime but used to drink between 6pm and 11pm every night between Sunday and Thursday and between 6pm and 1am every Friday and Saturday night, they would have an additional 39 hours a week spare by going completely dry. The fact that they would no longer have to recover from hangovers on Saturday and Sunday mornings would probably save them a further 10-12 hours a week.

> 'You will also have a huge amount of new time available which can, if you wish, be used for earning money.'

Over the course of an entire month they would therefore salvage around 220 hours, and if they used just half of these for moonlighting via a part-time job during the evenings and/or weekends that paid only the minimum wage, they would earn over £600 a month. £600 a month, invested every month in the average performing UK investment fund over the 30 years to the end of June 2007, would have become worth well over one and a half million pounds!

Few downsides

The lifestyle change created by becoming teetotal can be every bit as dramatic as changing career or relocating abroad but has fewer potential downsides. There are numerous people who have made the wrong career changes and who have ended up in an even worse rut than the one they started in. However, we are not aware of a single case of someone who has become a long-term teetotaller who does not claim to be happier than when they were drinking.

> "When people stop drinking they generally become much happier. I have personally found that you do have to change the way you live, but it's very freeing and the self-loathing dissipates."
>
> David Gilmour, Co-founder of specialist intermediary Re-cover

Many people develop drink problems because they have low self-esteem, but the act of becoming teetotal can provide that very self-esteem that was lacking. Giving up alcohol represents an amazing commitment to yourself and to the people you love most, and is something you can be rightly proud of and use as a foundation for rebuilding a new life.

Contrary to popular belief, the fact that you may then come across other people drinking virtually every day does not have to prove a source of temptation. Quite the opposite, it can actually serve as a constant reminder of your new sense of identity and of what you have achieved.

Stopping the rot

A further classic mistake made by many people with drink problems is to feel that they cannot change their drinking habits until they have discovered and tackled the underlying causes. But when a fireman is confronted with a fire he doesn't spend the first few hours trying to work out what has caused it. The immediate priority is to put out the fire, and the forensic analysis can follow later.

The term drink problem, like cancer, refers to literally hundreds of different conditions and each one has their own causes and individual solutions. Some people may drink excessively because they are lonely, unhappy or bored, whilst others may do so as a result of a genetic predisposition or an obsessive personality.

'The only statistic we care about is you. Whatever percentage of others have succeeded or failed to control their drinking is of no relevance.'

There is also some evidence to suggest that if younger women are heavy binge drinkers and also have eating disorders, it can be an indication that they have been abused or neglected in their childhood. And drink problems in younger men are often associated with hyperactivity in childhood. The list is endless.

Indeed, there is so much information out there that anyone with a drink problem who attempts to read everything written by every psycho-something-or-other is likely to be dead before they finish. If not, their brain will have become sufficiently addled to render the task futile.

'When a fireman is confronted with a fire, he doesn't spend the first few hours trying to work out what has caused it.'

The fact that leading experts and celebrity teetotallers commonly present wildly contrasting viewpoints, and often fail to acknowledge that any other opinion contains even an element of truth, only adds to the confusion. At one extreme there are those who maintain that everyone who has a drink problem has a disease, whilst at the other there are those who are equally adamant that anyone with a drink problem simply suffers from a lack of willpower.

Both camps are guilty of over-generalisation in the same way as someone who maintains that all cancers have the same cause and potential treatment solutions. What would be the point of treating someone for life-threatening leukaemia if they only had the very mildest form of skin cancer?

> **"But I'm not so think as you drunk I am."**
>
> J.C. Squire

The first step is to stop the rot by getting your drinking under control, and we strongly recommend giving up alcohol altogether, at least for an initial period. You then have the rest of your life in which to tackle the underlying causes of your drink problem and, as demonstrated by case studies in this book, once you have done this it may be possible to revert to drinking alcohol in a way that gives you far fewer problems. This does not necessarily mean suddenly stopping drinking with immediate effect. Indeed, if someone with a physical addiction tries to give up without medical advice it could prove fatal, or result in serious brain damage or memory loss.

If you become physically sick or start to have hallucinations if you don't have an alcoholic drink within a few hours of waking, you are suffering from the most serious kind of physical addiction and should seek medical advice immediately. If you can't get yourself to your GP or to the Accident and Emergency department of your local hospital, you should phone one of the numbers below to get help:

Numbers to ring for immediate help:

- NHS Direct: 0845 4647
- Drinkline: 0800 917 8282
- FRANK: 0800 776600

Medical detox

If someone who is physically addicted tries to give up without medical help, the withdrawal of alcohol will trigger their body into a state of emergency. This can burn up so much energy that memory loss or even death can result from the brain being deprived of vital vitamins. These risks, however, can be greatly reduced by the individual undergoing a medical detox, which involves being regularly administered drugs over a number of days or even weeks.

> 'If someone with a physical addiction tries to give up without medical help it could prove fatal or result in serious brain damage or memory loss.'

You don't have to be throwing up every five minutes or hallucinating about insects crawling all over the ceiling to have at least some degree of physical addiction. Many people are physically addicted without realising it. It is quite possible for someone who has a significant physical addiction to go through the whole of the working day without having had a drink since the night before. But by the time they get home, they will start to feel pretty agitated if they don't start drinking straight away. These agitation levels will start to die down within a quarter of an hour of having knocked back their first drink, and the drinking will then continue until they go to bed.

It is not unusual for drinkers who fit into this category to still be enjoying successful careers and to set great store by the fact that they are not alcoholics. "I only have a couple of drinks in the evening" is the classic defence. But problem drinkers commonly underestimate their drinking by at least half when confronted by a doctor, friend or family member, so "a couple" can easily mean three or four. Furthermore, the size of a "glass" of wine or spirits poured at home can easily be three or four times the size of a pub measure.

> "There is no such thing as a small whisky."
>
> Oliver St. John Gogarty

Other symptoms of physical addiction include experiencing a desire for alcohol first thing in the morning, sweating, shakiness, hiding alcohol from friends and family, and becoming increasingly moody and argumentative either whilst drinking or when drink is not available. Even those who merely experience minor anxiety, agitation or difficulty with sleep when they attempt to give up may have developed a physical addiction that warrants medical attention.

Anyone who suspects that they have any kind of physical addiction is strongly advised not to suddenly stop drinking without discussing the matter with a doctor or suitably qualified therapist first. Some who fail to do so may get away with giving up immediately, especially if they are still quite young, but others will cause themselves serious harm. It is simply not worth taking the risk.

If a medical detox is considered necessary, it doesn't necessarily have to involve being an inpatient in a hospital or private residential rehab clinic. In some cases it can be possible to receive treatment at home or simply to visit your GP, hospital or a specialist clinic on a regular basis.

> "Life is a broad church and I've had plenty of friends who have given up with AA or by themselves without a medical detox. But I think that if you are a bit shaky in the morning and feeling bad you may need to visit your GP to ask for help."
>
> Prof. Griffith Edwards, Emeritus Professor of Addiction Behaviour at the National Addiction Centre, Institute of Psychiatry, King's College London

Although a medical detox should help prevent those with physical addictions from causing themselves harm whilst withdrawing from drinking alcohol, completing such a process only constitutes winning the first battle. Overcoming a drink problem usually involves considerable willpower and may also necessitate understanding why you were drinking heavily in the first place – which could require getting treatment for psychological problems that caused you to do so.

Psychological addiction

Many problem drinkers do not have a physical addiction and will therefore experience no physical withdrawal symptoms when they don't drink. However, they may still have a psychological addiction. Someone who only has a psychological addiction does not require the assistance of a medical detox, and may be able to revert to controlled drinking again in the future.

But if a psychological addiction is not tackled, it can cause significant harm and is highly likely to lead to a physical addiction in the end because the body will gradually require more alcohol to create the same effect. The boundaries between when the former type of addiction leads to the latter are blurred, but the sooner the problem is addressed the better.

> **"You give up drinking when it is costing you more than money."**
>
> **Hugh Graham (See Case Study, Chapter 3, page 67)**

Classic signs of someone having a psychological addiction are if they often drink on their own, neglect other interests or pleasures in order to drink alcohol, prefer alcohol to their partners, feel guilty about their drinking or become unsettled if alcohol isn't readily available.

If asked about their drinking habits by family and friends, this type of drinker can be highly defensive on the subject, pointing out that they can't be addicted because they are able to give up for brief periods. But over a number of years, psychologically addicted drinkers will reach a stage when they can no longer give up for those brief periods without experiencing significant withdrawal symptoms, because they have also developed a physical addiction.

Help is at hand

Whatever form of drink problem you have, the good news is that you have the power within to overcome it. Around one third of problem drinkers manage to do so without any professional help at all, and the help options available are far greater than generally supposed. Some of these, such as treatment facilities funded by the NHS, social services and charitable bodies, and self-help groups like the AA, will cost you nothing, while many forms of private treatment cost less than you probably think. Even staying in private residential rehab doesn't have to involve the types of prices you may have seen splashed around in newspaper articles about celebrities visiting well known upmarket clinics. It can be possible to obtain a six-week residential rehab course followed up by three months of external counselling for around £6,000.

All you need is bottle!

Whatever help you receive, the war can only be won from within. Ultimately, victory depends primarily on one thing: You must want to overcome your drink problem more than you want to drink. Many people who have given up mainly for lifestyle reasons report that the process wasn't anything like as hard as they had first feared.

> "When I gave up drinking alcohol a lot of people said that it must be a real hardship. But on the Richter Scale of hardship it comes in at zero. Hardship is when you don't have access to safe drinking water, which over one billion people don't have."
>
> Helen Tirbutt, Co-author of "Beat The Booze"

The battle may prove considerably harder for those with psychological and physical addictions, but what the human resolve can achieve seems to know no bounds. Take, for example, the case of mountaineer Joe Simpson, whose experiences became the subject of the book and subsequent film "Touching The Void". Having faced almost certain death from hypothermia and dehydration when stranded high in the Andes with a broken leg, he somehow crawled to safety.

> "If you'd asked me before the event whether I could have done this I would have laughed you down, but we are capable of extraordinary things."
>
> Joe Simpson, Mountaineer and Author

Simpson has ended his motivational talks about his ordeal with the words: "We are all going to have a bad time in our lives. We are going to lose loved ones and jobs, and things are going to crash and burn. We will always wonder what it will be like and whether we will be brave enough and strong enough to cope."

"All I can do is assure you that you can draw depths of strength from both the mental and physical that I didn't believe were possible. If you'd asked me before the event whether I could have done this I would have laughed you down, but we are capable of extraordinary things."

In some ways your plight is far less severe than the one he experienced. You are not hoping for a passing helicopter to spot you and throw you a rope. Indeed, numerous easily accessible organisations and individuals detailed in this book are ready and willing to help you.

But in another respect you are more difficult to help. A freezing person stranded on a remote mountainside is not in the slightest doubt that they have a problem and need assistance, but you may still be in denial. In order to allow others to help, you must take that first all-important step of acknowledging that you have a drink problem. Trying to summon the courage to do so may feel as though you have a mountain to climb, but it is a decision that can be made in only an instant. There is so much help available that there is no reason why you should become stranded on the return journey to happiness.

Never too late

Remember also that it's never too late. Some case studies in this book did not conquer their drink problems until they reached their 50s and 60s. Even someone who doesn't give up until they reach their 70s or 80s will still be able to go to their grave knowing that they are a winner and that they will be remembered as such.

THINK BEFORE YOU DRINK

Department of Health Safe Drinking Guidelines

Men	Women
Men should drink no more than 21 units of alcohol per week (and no more than 3 or 4 units in one day).	Women should drink no more than 14 units of alcohol a week (and no more than 2 or 3 units in any one day).

What does this actually mean?

1 Unit = Roughly	1.5 Units = Roughly
• Half a pint of ordinary strength beer, lager or cider • A small pub measure of spirits • A standard pub measure of fortified pub wine like sherry or port	• A small glass of ordinary strength wine • A standard pub measure of spirits

(For more detailed information, see Appendix 1, page 202.)

* After an episode of heavy drinking it is advisable to stop drinking alcohol for 48 hours to allow your body to recover. This is not applicable for people who drink within the amounts recommended above.

* If you are planning to have a baby, or if you are pregnant, you should not drink.

Key points

- Delay equals deterioration

- Even if you are cutting down you should go completely dry for an initial spell

- Anyone with a physical addiction must not give up without a medical detox

- A wide range of free help is available

- Even private residential rehab can cost less than most people imagine

- You must want to overcome your drink problem more than you want to drink

- What the human resolve can achieve seems to know no bounds

Chapter 2:
Who Said Drinking Alcohol Was Cool?

Just as we tend to express astonishment at the way the ancient Romans were entertained by gladiators, archaeologists trying to make sense of current UK society in a few thousand years' time are more than likely to raise a few eyebrows at our drinking habits.

The fact that successive governments were actually encouraging a drinking culture that research demonstrated was causing harm to around a quarter of our adult population, would probably make "civilisation" seem a little too strong a word.

The alcohol industry has us over a barrel

All the evidence clearly shows that increasing the price of alcohol reduces consumption and therefore also reduces the harm that it causes. Yet, because UK governments have been reluctant to raise taxes, the price of alcohol relative to average incomes has halved since the mid 1960s. The situation is generally understood to reflect the lobbying power that the alcohol industry has with MPs. Anyone with a drink problem can therefore take some comfort from the knowledge that they are, to at least some extent, a victim of society.

A sobering thought

Please don't think we are party poopers. To the majority of people who have no difficulty in controlling their drinking, our advice is simply to enjoy themselves. But it doesn't take a genius to work out that if any other pastime that harmed a quarter of the adult population was invented today it would be instantly banned.

The fact that some illegal drugs cause far less harm than alcohol also represents an absurd situation. Indeed, the Home Office has even been warned by its own senior advisers that alcohol is more harmful than the Class A drugs LSD and ecstasy.

> **"I wonder whether the current alcohol strategy was written by the Government for the alcohol industry or by the alcohol industry for the Government."**
>
> **Dr. Francis Keaney, Consultant Addiction Psychiatrist, National Addiction Centre, Institute of Psychiatry, King's College London**

Problem drinkers are effectively paying the price of the widespread availability of a drug that should, in theory, be illegal. It will clearly never be made illegal in practice, but it should at least be sold at a price that makes affordability a much more serious issue.

Problem drinkers are having to live in a society in which many people don't seem to be able to envisage having a good time without getting completely wrecked, and the failure of successive governments to implement the necessary tax increases has contributed towards this situation. When people went out to have a good time in the 1960s, alcohol was sometimes a part of it, but it was not normally the focus.

> "I grew up at a time when we met in coffee bars, but now it's wine bars, and many young people go there with the simple intention of getting drunk."
>
> Esther Rantzen, Founder of ChildLine

This attitude is also completely out of sync with those prevalent in many other parts of the world. Millions of Muslims and members of other religions that prohibit or discourage alcohol seem to have no problems in enjoying themselves whilst sober. As you will see from the case study of Claire Bannister (See Chapter 4, page 73), attending a Muslim wedding where there are only soft drinks available can be an exhilarating experience.

Even European countries where drinking is widespread can have a totally different attitude towards drunkenness.

> "Italians are appalled and bewildered at English drunkenness. To them, public drunkenness is as unacceptable as evacuating your bowels in your underpants."
>
> John Fraser (See Case Study, Chapter 3, page 56)

But being a victim of society doesn't mean that you have a licence to indulge in self-pity. The simple truth is that society isn't going to change for a very long time. We have seen how sense has finally prevailed with other outmoded harmful practices, such as drinking and driving, heavy lunchtime drinking by business people and smoking in public places. We have also experienced some recent glimmers of hope, such as the announcement that alcoholic drinks will carry new health warning labels by the end of 2008, and government proposals to review 24 hour drinking and combat underage alcohol consumption.

There will hopefully come a time when someone who is throwing up with a hangover is regarded as suffering from poisoning rather than viewed as a source of amusement, and when those who regularly get drunk at social gatherings start becoming perceived as social misfits. But it is likely to take the best part of a generation to alter the mindset, and any problem drinker who waits for such a new dawn to break may well fail to live to see the day.

Time for a brief biology lesson

Alcohol is soaked up through the lining of the stomach and intestines and is absorbed into the bloodstream, hence the conventional wisdom that if you first line the stomach with a good meal it can help prevent alcohol from "going to your head".

In small doses, alcohol can reduce inhibitions and induce a general sense of well-being. There is even evidence to suggest that extremely moderate drinking (of around a glass of wine a day) by middle-aged and older people can reduce the risk of having a heart attack or stroke and is associated with healthy ageing. However, it is no good trying to use this potential health benefit as an excuse for excessive drinking. There is no evidence to suggest that drinking more than such modest amounts is good for your health, and plenty of evidence to show that drinking significantly more can cause very serious health problems.

Continuous heavy drinking of alcohol starts to affect your speech, balance, physical co-ordination and mental judgement. The exact impact that it will have on external behaviour will vary from one individual to another. It may make some people sleepy, while it can make others violent. But internally, they are likely to have a lot in common; their livers will be working overtime.

It's a hard life being a liver

Your liver is responsible for processing the alcohol you drink and eliminating it from the body by breaking it down into water, gas and fat. But this is only one of hundreds of important jobs it has to do, so it starts experiencing considerable strain if you drink heavily. It essentially has to start doing overtime if you drink more than about half a pint of beer or its equivalent an hour.

Just as some employees who are continuously asked to work unreasonable hours handle the strain better than others, no two livers can be guaranteed to react to the excess demands placed on them in exactly the same way. The difference between a disgruntled employee and a disgruntled liver is that the employee is likely to make their feelings known at a relatively early stage.

'It doesn't take a genius to work out that if any other pastime that harmed a quarter of the adult population was invented today it would be instantly banned.'

If you accidentally put your finger on an oven hotplate, you are likely to take it away again pretty quickly. Unfortunately, the liver has no such built-in safety mechanism because it has very few nerve ends. It is therefore quite possible that a problem drinker will not experience any physical pain until they have entered the final stages of alcoholic liver disease, by which time it could be too late to make a recovery.

For this reason it is important that anyone who suspects they have been drinking too heavily for a prolonged period should seek medical advice. Trying to feel your liver at the bottom of your rib cage is unlikely to tell you anything, but doctors can detect damage by using blood tests and, if required, scans.

"As a GP you are well placed to tackle issues in relation to problem drinking. Evidence shows that simple screening tests used in the consultation can detect individuals drinking hazardously or harmfully. Once identified, providing timely advice on how to cut down and supporting individuals to adopt healthier drinking patterns can reduce the risk of alcohol related disease such as hypertension, depression and liver disease."

Dr. Linda Harris, Director of the Royal College of General Practitioners Substance Misuse Unit

Fortunately, if liver damage can be spotted early enough it can normally be reversed, because most livers are sufficiently tough to withstand serious abuse by replacing damaged cells with healthy ones. Two or three years of very heavy drinking, or 10 to 20 years of drinking slightly over the government's recommended guidelines, can cause significant damage without being accompanied by any symptoms. Although, if you then stop drinking or cut down to safe levels, the liver may be able to carry on working.

There is, however, always the danger that the liver will eventually conclude that enough is enough. The final stages of liver disease occur when it finally runs out of healthy cells and develops cirrhosis. (We make no apologies for including this term in our jargon-free pages because any problem drinker who hasn't heard of it must have been living on Planet Zog.)

"We drink one another's health, and spoil our own."

Jerome K. Jerome

Once it has developed cirrhosis, your liver can't recover, although you can prevent further damage and increase your chances of survival if you stop drinking.

Lethal cocktail

In the very final stages of cirrhosis, the liver becomes so damaged that the whole body becomes poisoned by waste products which the liver has become unable to deal with. This will lead to the failure of other major organs, which is likely to prove fatal. In some cases a liver transplant may be possible to prevent cirrhosis from proving a death sentence, but this is only likely to be granted if the individual concerned remains completely dry for at least six months beforehand.

> "Everybody with an addiction problem quits eventually. And yes, many of them do it on their own. When they die from cirrhosis or wrapping their car around a tree."
>
> Anonymous contributor to Addictions.co.uk website

The possibility of developing cirrhosis of the liver is the ultimate deterrent for the heavy drinker, but not all those with a drink problem will suffer from it, just as not all smokers will get lung cancer. Indeed, research suggests that no more than around a third of heavy drinkers will suffer this fate.

Someone who tries to take a cavalier approach towards life may decide that such a risk is worth taking, and declaring to your mates that you have to die of something may sound very macho to some people. But it would register as decidedly "uncool" to anyone who has ever experienced paying a hospital visit to someone suffering from cirrhosis. The final stages of liver disease can involve spending many weeks in agony. Seeing someone who has turned bright yellow, has tubes sticking out of virtually every orifice and is hallucinating to an extent that they cannot even recognise longstanding friends, is likely to be a life-changing experience for most people.

More than a tissue issue

It's not as though those who feel the risks of developing cirrhosis are worth taking are playing a game of Russian roulette. There will be no instant bullet through the brain for the losers, and there are no winners – because drink can harm you in around a hundred other ways (see Appendix 1). But anyone who is unmoved by the threat of cirrhosis is unlikely to be too deterred by the grizzly details of the numerous other long-term health risks, including the much publicised link between drinking alcohol and breast cancer. They should therefore focus instead on some of the more immediate consequences of drinking.

Many experts in the field stress that the risk of personal accidents faced by those with drink problems are amongst the most serious causes of potential concern after liver damage.

> "Brain damage is common and gradual, and you can cause harm well before you suffer advanced dementia. I would place physical accidents, like falling down the stairs or getting involved in brawls or punch-ups, high on the list as well, along with despair and the vastly increased risk of suicide."
>
> Prof. Griffiths Edwards, Emeritus Professor of Addiction Behaviour at the National Addiction Centre, Institute of Psychiatry, King's College London

Even those who are absolutely determined to ignore long-term health risks and "live for today" should seriously question how much actual "living" they will be doing in a life that is dominated by alcohol consumption. If you wish to be attractive to the opposite sex, for example, you need a drink problem like you need a hole in the head.

Fatal lack of attraction

Yes, drink can break down inhibitions on those early dates, but the impact it has on both sexes is unlikely to prove too romantic in the long run. Indeed, drinking to excess is one of the quickest ways of losing a partner and one of the surest ways of finding that you don't meet a suitable new one.

Clearly it can be awkward to be asked why you are not drinking at all during an early date, but as we discuss in Chapter 3 (See page 44), there are many reasons you can give other than volunteering that you used to have a drink problem. Once a worthwhile relationship has been established, there should be no problem with coming clean on the subject.

Macduff: "What three things does drink especially provoke?"

Porter: "Marry, sir, nose-painting, sleep and urine. Lechery, sir it provokes and unprovokes: It provokes the desire, but it takes away the performance."

William Shakespeare ("Macbeth")

In addition to experiencing the dreaded brewer's droop and a loss of sex drive, men who drink heavily can actually suffer from a shrinkage in the size of their penis and testicles, impotency and a loss of pubic hair. If they develop cirrhosis they may even start developing enlarged breasts. Women with drink problems can develop menstrual irregularities, shrinkage of the breasts, failure to ovulate and sexual difficulties.

> "Drinking affects the liver and the skin hugely. The body has to get rid of the toxins and the skin is a key elimination organ."
>
> Teresa Hale, Founder of The Hale Clinic, London

Apart from the obvious risks of throwing up in front of – or all over – a loved one, or being permanently skint as a result of being unable to hold down a job, other turn-off triggers commonly produced by heavy drinking for both sexes include a blotchy complexion, skin disorders and putting on weight – because alcohol contains plenty of calories but has almost no nutritional value.

Losing one inhibition too many

Add in the ability of drunkenness to lead to unsafe sex, to create temptation towards two-timing a partner, and to leave women vulnerable to rape and sexual assault, and you already have a pretty horrendous cocktail of potential tragedy.

> "One more drink and I'd have been under the host."
>
> Dorothy Parker

The emotional strain that heavy drinking can place on relationships can also be every bit as costly. At one end of the scale it can play a significant part in many divorces and cases of domestic violence and child abuse. At the other end it can merely prevent couples from being as happy as they would ideally like to be. Regular drinking can make you feel tired and depressed and difficult to get on with, especially if you are unwilling to acknowledge that you have any form of drink problem, and getting drunk often involves betraying the confidences of those closest to you.

> 'Teetotallers often make ideal friends and partners because they never let out secrets when they are drunk.'

Additionally, the drinking habits of parents can be a major factor behind drink problems developed by their children (See Chapter 7), and there is increasing evidence that drinking of any sort during pregnancy can harm unborn children. Indeed, the latest governmental guidance is that women should refrain from drinking any alcohol at all during pregnancy.

Those who refuse to address their own drink problems but who insist on skimping and saving to send their children to private school or to buy a house in the catchment area of a good State school, should therefore surely be asking whether they have their priorities right in their quest to provide their children with the best possible start in life.

Key points

- If you have a drink problem you are, to some extent, a victim of society

- But society won't change in time to help you

- Your liver starts working overtime if you drink more than half a pint of beer an hour

- You may not feel any physical pain until it is too late

- If liver damage can be spotted early enough it can normally be reversed

- Problem drinkers are far more likely than average to suffer accidents

- They are also more likely to experience weight problems and skin disorders

Chapter 3:
Giving Up Alcohol Completely

If you have a drink problem, you have a straight choice between doing something about it now or spending the rest of your life worrying about it. There is no middle ground, because failure to confront the problem is effectively making the latter choice. The issue will not suddenly go away. Logically, the decision should be a "no-brainer" because, whatever your philosophy of life, you are unlikely to disagree that it is better to be happy than unhappy.

> 'We are not aware of a single case of someone who has become a long-term teetotaller who does not claim to be happier than when they were drinking.'

But ending any long-term relationship is rarely easy in the early stages. Just as when splitting up with a long-term romantic partner, you must first be clear in your own mind that the move is the only realistic solution going forward. You must then find the sheer bloody-mindedness not to let anyone else or any future meetings with your previous partner persuade you otherwise – and you will come across this particular previous partner often enough!

Breaking up is hard to do

As with ending any relationship, the first few months will be the most difficult. Old habits die hard, and you will find yourself with a lot more time on your hands than you had before. The support network that you have around you could therefore prove crucial. In a similar way to when someone is going through a divorce or separating from a long-term partner, you are likely to require considerable contact with immediate family and close friends in the short-term.

> 'Ultimately, victory depends primarily on one thing: You must want to overcome your drink problem more than you want to drink.'

In the longer term, the ultimate solution to any break-up is likely to be to find a new partner. In the case of someone giving up the drink, it is going to have to be a very different kind of partner to the one with whom they have previously been involved. A new hobby, sport or work goal can often fill the void, as can membership of AA or another self-help group.

Additionally, those who give up alcohol will also have to make a physical recovery in the early months. Indeed, it can often take up to a year, or in some cases even twice this length of time, before you are once again functioning at your optimum.

> "I had been drinking heavily for 20 years and after giving up I reckoned my mental capabilities improved every month for at least two years."
>
> **Hugh Graham (See Case Study, Chapter 3, page 67)**

Once you have got the first couple of years under your belt, things should become a lot easier. You should feel immeasurably healthier and happier and have started to function on something of an automatic pilot. Just as when you begin to learn to ride a bicycle, you are likely to have to concentrate very hard at first and will probably need the support of other people. Eventually you will be able to do it almost without thinking, because it has become habit – and if you suffer from a drink problem you don't need reminding of how powerful habits can become. You are effectively substituting one habit for another.

> "Just as you acquire a taste for a life with alcohol, you can acquire a taste for a life without it. After a certain period, you will find that it becomes your automatic reaction to say no to alcohol – just as it may have been your automatic reaction to always say yes in the past."
>
> Helen Tirbutt, Co-author of "Beat The Booze"

After a couple of years you should also have won the respect of most worthwhile individuals around you, because they will see that your desire to give up was not merely idle talk. Most people like a winner, and by then that is what you will be perceived as. But don't be put off by those who are envious.

> 'Some teetotallers will tell you that if they have one major problem it is having to deal with jealousy from other people.'

You may be able to give up drinking without professional help, but if you need such help (the options for which are outlined in detail in Chapter 5) the information contained in the current chapter can still be used in conjunction with it.

Downing the drink

Similarly, if you have had a psychological addiction, you may decide that you want to try to revert to drinking in moderation at some stage in the future (detailed information on cutting down is provided in Chapter 4). The current chapter can still help you achieve that initial period of being dry that is so essential in enabling you to sort out your underlying problems.

> "Our basic approach is to get people off the drink first and then try to find the underlying reasons. They may or may not discover what has been causing their drinking but, even if they don't find out, they will still be happier from not drinking and more able to cope."
>
> David Ball, Senior Lecturer at the Institute of Psychiatry (See Chapter 5, page 106)

Can you ever drink again?

Most addiction experts volunteer the same broad rules of thumb with regard to whether it is possible for a problem drinker to ever drink again. If you have only a psychological addiction, it may be possible to revert to drinking again in moderation in the future, providing you give up altogether for a significant period of time – during which you resolve the underlying problems that were causing you to drink. If, on the other hand, you have had a physical addiction, you should never touch another drop.

Even if someone with a physical addiction gives up for as long as 30 years, as soon as they have another drink they will almost certainly start drinking to excess again. Indeed, within days of having that first drink they are likely to be consuming alcohol at the same levels they did before they originally gave up. This is because your brain permanently alters its attitude towards alcohol when you have a physical addiction. However long you stop for, as soon as you have that first drink your brain will recognise the smell, taste, and sensation of alcohol! It will immediately readjust itself and you will find that you are largely powerless to stop yourself drinking far more than you had intended.

> "I don't think many experts would disagree that someone who has been severely dependent should never drink again."
>
> Prof. Chris Cook, Professorial Research Fellow at Durham University

Whilst there are always the odd exceptions to this rule (See Case Study of Hugh Graham, page 67), experts tend to suggest that they must never have had a physical addiction in the first place.

How do you tell if you have a physical addiction?

As discussed in Chapter 1 (see pages 11 and 12), those with a physical addiction will experience withdrawal symptoms within a few hours of stopping drinking. These can range from being physically sick and hallucinating, to wanting to drink alcohol first thing in the morning, sweating, shakiness and becoming increasingly moody and argumentative – both whilst drinking and when drink is not available. You may have even developed a physical addiction if you merely find yourself becoming anxious or agitated or are having difficulty sleeping. But the boundaries between psychological and physical addiction are somewhat blurred.

'It is quite possible for someone who has a significant physical addiction to go through the whole of the working day without having had a drink since the night before.'

Anyone who is not sure whether they have a physical addiction should seek expert advice, and they do not necessarily have to pay for this. You can discuss the issue with your GP or with the helpers manning any of the helpline services detailed in Chapter 1 (See page 11). In some areas, you will also have the option of simply turning up at a local community alcohol and drug service during the relevant opening hours (See Chapter 5, pages 105-107). Even some private treatment services offer initial free advice up to a certain level. Some of the specialist intermediaries detailed in Chapter 5 (See page 112) are willing to discuss such issues over the telephone, and The Priory Group will even provide a free, no-obligation initial face-to-face consultation at one of its 14 clinics (See Appendix 3, page 234).

Do you need a medical detox?

Establishing whether you have a physical addiction is not only vital for the purposes of knowing whether you can ever drink alcohol again, it is also essential for finding out whether you need help with the actual physical withdrawal process via a medical detox – replacing alcohol with other drugs in doses that reduce over a number of days (See Chapter 1, pages 12 to 14).

'If someone with a physical addiction tries to give up without medical help it could prove fatal or result in serious brain damage or memory loss.'

Some people won't need a medical detox even if they have been drinking five pints of beer – or its equivalent – a day; although that certainly doesn't mean that they haven't been causing themselves harm. Nevertheless, what one person can get away with can prove fatal to others. In particular, the older we get the more susceptible we become to damage from withdrawal.

Someone in their 20s or 30s might be able to give up without undergoing a medical detox or experiencing withdrawal symptoms after drinking amounts that would kill a middle-aged person if they tried to do the same. So you should definitely seek advice if you are unsure whether you have a physical addiction or not. Even those who are reasonably certain that they don't require a medical detox should leave nothing to chance by cutting down their drinking very gradually over a period of weeks rather than giving up immediately. They may also benefit from taking multi-vitamin supplements whilst doing so.

> **"People shouldn't give up without professional help if they have a poor state of nutrition or a history of epilepsy or of hallucinating when stopping drinking."**
>
> **Dr. Mike McPhillips, Consultant Psychiatrist and Lead Addiction Treatment Consultant at the Priory Hospital, Roehampton**

Depending on the area you live in, it may be possible to obtain a medical detox at your GP's surgery, at a local alcohol and drug community service, or possibly even at the Accident and Emergency unit of your local NHS hospital. (See Chapter 5, pages 105 to 106.) It can also be possible to pay to have a medical detox administered privately at home or whilst in a residential rehab clinic, and in some circumstances – if you are considered to be trustworthy and to have a very supportive family or partner – you may even be allowed to administer your own medical detox at home.

But wherever the detox takes place, it is essential that you are completely honest with those who administer it about how much you've been drinking. If, for example, you have given a misleading picture of your drinking habits on your application form for admittance to a residential rehab clinic because you thought it might increase your chances of acceptance, it is vital that you come clean at this point. Failure to do so could have very serious consequences for your health.

Silence isn't always golden

Before you actually begin the giving up process, you must address the issue of whether you want the fact that you are recovering from a drink problem to be public knowledge or to be kept a secret within your immediate family and closest circle of friends.

It is most commonly argued that it is best not to try to hide the fact because half the battle is admitting that you have a problem, and trying to conceal it from anyone is merely adding to your denial. You are usually much more effective at being yourself than at pretending to be anyone else, and the fact that you used to have a drink problem and that you no longer drink alcohol will represent a significant part of yourself from now onwards.

Many people are concerned that rumours about them having a drink problem could find their way back to their workplace, but the chances are that work colleagues will have noticed that all has not been well for some time. Furthermore, many employers will be highly supportive of employees who admit to having drink problems.

"We tell people that the start of the process is admitting you have a problem and going to your employer and letting them know that you are ill. You don't have to be specific about your illness, but you do need to tell them as soon as possible. Remember that research shows that somewhere between a sixth and a quarter of the population has a drink problem of some sort and, who knows, your boss could even be an addict in recovery."

Keith Burns, Managing Director of independent advice and referral agency ADMIT Services

The first step in assessing your employer's potential attitude should be to see if it has a written alcohol policy (See Chapter 9). If it does have one, this is likely to state that it has a policy of supporting those who volunteer drink problems and ask for help, and any such pledge should be taken at face value. Your employer may give you free counselling or other treatment or advice via an internal or external occupational health department, and may even pay for you to spend several weeks in a private residential rehab clinic.

Even if your employer isn't prepared to pay for rehab, it may bend over backwards to give you the necessary time off to fund such treatment yourself, and to ensure that you are made to feel extremely welcome on your return and are able to resume your career with as little interruption as possible.

CASE STUDY: SOBER 'TIL THE DAY I DIE

When a family member offered to pay for 45-year-old Thomas Page to go to a residential rehab clinic in 2005, he laughed at the suggestion.

Despite dry-vomiting every morning, sipping from a brandy bottle at work every afternoon and getting wrecked every evening, he was in total denial. Even an official warning from his employer had failed to make any impression.

But after hitting a "nasty rock bottom" in March 2006, he summoned the courage to take up the offer and spent six weeks at the Clouds House residential rehab clinic in Wiltshire. Here, he learned via the 12 Step programme that he will never be able to drink again, and he has attended AA regularly since leaving.

> 'Even if I learned I only had six months to live I would never drink again because I would want to enjoy those six months to the full.'

Thomas, who works in the office furniture industry, says "I don't think I could have done it without the support of both organisations. Going to Clouds House physically kept me away from the drink for six weeks in a secure cotton wool environment, and made me realise that many other people had addictions as bad as my own. But AA is important on an ongoing basis and I attend it most days."

"The support shown to me by my family and friends and employer has also been vital. When I told work I needed six weeks off to sort things out, everyone said it was a brilliant idea and made it clear that there would still be a job for me."

Thomas describes himself as a "completely different person, who is much happier and gets up every morning grateful to be alive". When he has a problem he now deals with it immediately rather than drowning his sorrows and allowing it to escalate. Work has been going far better since he became sober, and he has even managed to negotiate an amicable divorce without relapsing.

"I have still had times when I have thought that I could blot it all out, but I have never been tempted because I have learned in a totally rational way that drinking will make things worse," he continues. "Even if I learned I only had six months to live I would never drink again because I would want to enjoy those six months to the full."

'I have never been tempted because I have learned in a totally rational way that drinking will make things worse.'

But there is still one thing that, given the benefit of hindsight, Thomas would have done differently in his battle against the booze. In the week before entering Clouds House he stopped drinking altogether without the help of a medical detox, and he is probably lucky to still be alive.

"I had the most terrible withdrawal symptoms and ended up in my local Accident and Emergency unit," he recalls. "I was sweating and shaking terribly and my vision often switched to black and white, so anyone with a serious problem should seek medical advice before giving up."

What if you are unemployed?

Even those who have not had a job for some time and do not wish to conceal former drink problems should not find it an insurmountable problem to get back on the employment ladder if they are able to demonstrate they have put their problems behind them. Many employers are enlightened enough to realise that former problem drinkers who have been dry for any significant length of time make better than average workers (See Chapter 9, page 192). Apart from anything else, those who make enough applications are, by the law of averages, bound to find that some of them are dealt with by other former addicts.

But anyone who finds they are getting nowhere should try applying to some of the residential rehab clinics themselves (See Appendix 3). Many of these clinics make a point of employing reformed drinkers in all areas of their workforces – from therapists and administrative staff to kitchen staff and cleaners.

A few white lies

Despite the perceived wisdom of not concealing your drink problem, there are inevitably certain situations, both socially and in a business environment, in which you may prefer not to go into detail about your previous drinking habits. It can, for example, be extremely tedious to be constantly grilled on the matter by people you have never seen before and are unlikely to meet again.

> "Who former drinkers tell about their previous problem and when they tell them is a very personal decision and depends very much on the circumstances concerned and who they are talking to."
>
> Rick Weeks, Business Director at Broadreach House

There is also a danger of appearing "holier than thou" in some situations, and this can prove a real problem for teetotallers because other people do not normally take kindly to being corrected or advised on how to lead their life (See Case Study of Claire Bannister, Chapter 4, page 73).

There is therefore no harm in keeping a few white lies up your sleeve to deal with awkward situations. Useful "get out" phrases include: "I started developing terrible hangovers, so I don't touch a drop now"; "It irritates my stomach"; "I started getting a terrible reaction"; "I used to be allergic".

> **"If you have an excuse that's fully plausible it doesn't have to completely satisfy other people. It's not really any of their business."**
>
> Prof. Michael O'Donnell, Chief Medical Officer at Unum

You may also wish to consider whether you want details of any drink problem to appear on your medical records and run the risk of it coming back to haunt to you in the future when you apply for a job or insurance policy. If you are particularly concerned about this issue, you may prefer to sidestep your GP and obtain private treatment directly (See Chapter 5, page 100).

However, such a step should never be taken lightly because many GPs can be invaluable in the early stages of combating a drink problem. In addition to providing constant moral support, they can help you assess the seriousness of your problem, establish whether you need a medical detox and – if applicable – arrange for this to be carried out, and refer you to appropriate counselling and other treatment services.

As long as you have actually stopped drinking, GPs can also help you by administering drugs that reduce alcohol withdrawal cravings and help you stay sober. If sleeping pills become necessary during the withdrawal process, they can also prescribe these.

The early weeks

Regardless of whether or not you have needed a medical detox, you can greatly increase your chances of remaining dry during the early weeks and months by taking plenty of exercise and eating a healthy diet. Exercise can provide a useful distraction, as well as helping to keep clean the blood supply and the liver. Walking, jogging and swimming can be ideal for the purpose, but experts stress the importance of only doing them in moderation and sticking to a form of exercise you are already familiar with.

How long it takes to feel well again will vary according to the length and severity of the addiction. Those with mild psychological dependencies could find it takes only a few weeks or a few days, but those with physical addictions are more likely to find that it takes between three months and a year.

Don't worry if you don't sleep well during the first two or three weeks as this is quite normal and, if you are eating a healthy diet and your body is being refreshed with nutrients, you are unlikely to feel that tired as a result.

WHAT SHOULD I EAT?

Dirk Budka, microbiologist, nutritionist and allergologist, advises keeping a diet diary every day and writing down in it everything you eat and drink.

"If you have had a day when you craved alcohol, then maybe you had something that contributed to this, like sugar or chocolate," he explains. "It's completely wrong to have sweets and fizzy drinks because they have similar sugars to those in alcoholic drinks. It is best to eat foods that fit in with a good liver cleansing programme, such as fruit and vegetables and whole grains like brown rice, couscous, buck wheat and quinoa."

"These have the right kind of sugars to convert to something useful, and will help to reduce cravings as well as to repair your liver. Your best chance is always to keep your liver completely clean and, as long as you don't have cirrhosis, you can restore it within a year to being completely normal."

Dirk also believes that a good Vitamin C supplement can help you fight liver damage and generally bolster your immune system, and he highlights the importance of increasing your intake of food rich in Magnesium and Vitamin B.

"Have food strong in these like seeds, nuts, broccoli and cauliflower, or take vitamin supplements for a period of time," he continues. "Avoid artificial sweeteners because they are much stronger than sugar. Your taste buds warn your stomach that there's a lot of sugar coming down, so your stomach releases chemicals to reduce the sugar, but these then have nothing to do and can therefore increase your craving for sugar. So the brain feels that it needs sugar or alcohol."

(For contact details for Dirk Budka see Appendix 3, page 264.)

Lifestyle considerations

Experts disagree about whether those who give up drinking should also give up smoking at the same time. There is evidence to suggest that someone who continues to smoke can have an increased risk of relapsing back into problem drinking but there is also a lot to be said for not trying to do too much at once.

> **"People get very contradictory advice about whether they should also give up smoking, but I tend to advise giving up one at a time as doing both at once is very hard."**
>
> **Mike McPhillips, Consultant Psychiatrist and Lead Addiction Treatment Consultant at The Priory Hospital, Roehampton**

There is no point in trying to kid yourself that drink isn't going to be around and, as discussed in Chapter 1, many people who have successfully given up alcohol actually get a buzz out of continually coming across other people drinking, because it reminds them what a fantastic feat they have achieved. This feeling of superiority does, however, inevitably take time to develop, as the first step is to prove to yourself and others that you can actually remain dry.

There is therefore much to be said for organising your life around activities that don't involve drink during the first couple of years. In extreme cases this could even necessitate a change of career. If, for example, you are working as a bar man (See Case Study of Jason Hendry, Chapter 6, page 124), or in a business development role that is highly dependent on attending boozy lunches, it clearly may not be ideal.

New pastimes

You should consider reverting to pastimes you used to enjoy before your drink problem started taking over, or even taking up entirely new hobbies. If you have an obsessive personality, a tried and tested solution is to get obsessed by a new pastime that is much healthier than drinking.

"Ted Nye describes running as his 'new bottle'. The 45-year-old journalist realised that the only realistic way for someone with his type of 'all or nothing personality' to get his drinking under control was to become obsessed with a healthier pastime."

Ted Nye (See Case Study, Chapter 4, page 82)

Even if you are a more laid-back type of individual, there is a lot to be said for doing things at certain times of the day when you would have drunk, like joining a dance or literature class. Don't worry if you don't enjoy it too much to start with, because the enjoyment often doesn't start kicking in for several months. Attending meditation classes or listening to meditation tapes at home is also highly recommended, as is having alternative therapies such as reflexology, Indian head massages and Reiki.

"Alcohol is a mind changing substance that is often used by people to 'relieve' stress and tension. In fact, there are many other things a person can turn to, which are much more effective and healthy than alcohol. For example, any form of meditation is an excellent means of achieving a more peaceful state of mind."

Nic Whitham, Director, Banyan Retreat Healing Centre, Near Ashford, Kent

In some cases, those who have given up drinking altogether can benefit from the new range of de-alcoholised wines and beers that have started to become available during recent years (See Chapter 4, pages 87 and 88). But whilst these can taste far superior to the traditional non-alcoholic offerings that have been widely available in supermarkets, it is debateable whether it is wise to simulate your old drinking habits. This type of drink is therefore arguably far more suitable for those who are cutting down, or for pregnant women or others who are giving up for only a limited period.

Unhealthy scepticism

It is important to realise that those around you will not always react in quite the way you had hoped or expected when you triumphantly reveal that you have given up drinking forever. Even though it may be clear in your own mind that you will achieve what you have announced, other people are likely to greet the news with a certain amount of scepticism at first.

The reaction from partners can, in particular, fall way short of what you had expected until you have established some clear blue water between your old self, the problem drinker, and your new self, the teetotaller. You may find that where you are expecting praise you are merely getting encouragement, and this can sometimes seem terribly patronising. But if you have a partner who had been urging you to give up drinking, at least they should be supportive in principle, even if they reserve euphoric praise for a year or two.

> "It's common for people to be less happy in the first few weeks and months after they have given up because, if they have a partner, they are always expecting them to be rushing around hugging them. But the partner may be sceptical that anything has really changed, and they are not going to believe it until it really happens."
>
> Dr. Duncan Raistrick, Consultant Addiction Psychiatrist

Fair-weather friends

Unfortunately, however, support will not always be so forthcoming from those who have purported to be "friends". Some friends will be offended that you are not prepared to make an exception to your resolution whilst you are with them. Others will go a step further and accuse you of being a "bore". Unsurprisingly, many such individuals invariably show the classic symptoms, described in Chapter 1, of having either a psychological or physical addiction.

It is important to realise that they are the ones with the problem, not you. It is human nature for those with problems to seek comfort in numbers and all these people are effectively trying to do is reduce you to their own level.

> "The only ones who look down on former drinkers tend to be those who have serious drink problems themselves. Knocking someone who is teetotal is a way of hiding their own problems."
>
> Rick Weeks, Business Director at Broadreach House

The majority of people who don't have any alcohol dependency themselves are, however, likely to be far more respectful to your predicament.

Dating and relationships

Even if you start dating someone, there is no reason why they should have a problem with you if you are honest enough to admit upfront that you used to drink too much and have done something about it.

"Most women probably wouldn't be bothered by a man who was honest enough to admit upfront that they used to have a drink problem, but they would be bothered by someone who was getting drunk a lot."

Fran Keen, Nurse at Broadway Lodge residential rehab clinic

Whilst there will inevitably be exceptions to this rule, you just have to accept that those individuals will not make compatible partners, in the same way that others will not be suitable on the grounds of other criteria. However, it takes a long time for someone recovering from a serious drink problem to have enough energy to sustain a relationship, and it is worth waiting until you have been dry for a year. This will also mean that you can offer a new partner the credibility of at least some track record of sobriety.

'Even though it may be clear in your own mind that you will achieve what you have announced, other people are likely to greet the news with a certain amount of scepticism at first.'

Aim to be bubbly

Try not to talk about your previous drink problem too much whilst out on dates, because it is unlikely to ever be as interesting a subject of conversation to your date as it is to you. Finding another interest to replace the drinking can certainly count positive in this respect by helping to lighten you up and broaden your range of conversation.

Even if you are pleased with the support you are receiving from those around you, loneliness is still likely to be a big issue because your remaining social circle will probably be a lot narrower than the one that you enjoyed before you developed your drink problem. But joining a self-help group can go a long way towards combating this (for contact details for AA, SMART Recovery UK and SOS International, see Appendix 3).

Alcoholics Anonymous

AA is by far the largest and best known of such self-help groups, and wherever you live there is likely to be a local group that meets regularly. The only requirement for joining is a desire to stop drinking. There is no fee payable, you can attend meetings anonymously as and when you like, and your involvement will not be recorded on your medical records. AA is essentially a fellowship of men and women who share experiences, strengths and hopes with each other in order to solve their common problem and help others with drink problems.

"AA is everywhere and is the biggest club in the world. Wherever you go you can attend a meeting where everyone will understand you because they are alcoholics."

Peter Davis, Counsellor at Broadway Lodge residential rehab clinic

There are two common types of AA meetings: open meetings and closed meetings. The former are open to those with drink problems and their families and to anyone interested in helping someone else with a drink problem. A chairperson usually describes the AA programme briefly for the benefit of newcomers and introduces one or more other speakers, who relate their personal drinking histories. A hat is normally passed to cover expenses and informal discussions often take place over light refreshments at the end.

Closed AA meetings are, on the other hand, limited to those with drink problems. They provide an opportunity for members to share with one another problems relating to drinking patterns and attempts to achieve sustainable sobriety. They also permit detailed discussion of various elements of the recovery programme.

The relative success of the AA programme owes a great deal to the fact that those who have managed to conquer drink problems have an exceptional faculty for getting through to, and helping, others who still have drink problems. The heart of the suggested programme of personal recovery is contained in the 12 Steps, which describe the experience of the earliest members of the Society.

THE 12 STEPS OF AA

1. We admitted we were powerless over alcohol – that our lives had become unmanageable.

2. Came to believe that a Power greater than ourselves could restore us to sanity.

3. Made a decision to turn our will and our lives over to the care of God as we understood Him.

4. Made a searching and fearless moral inventory of ourselves.

5. Admitted to God, to ourselves and to another human being the exact nature of our wrongs.

6. Were entirely ready to have God remove all these defects of character.

7. Humbly asked Him to remove our shortcomings.

8. Made a list of all persons we had harmed, and became willing to make amends to them all.

9. Made direct amends to such people wherever possible, except when to do so would injure them or others.

10. Continued to take personal inventory and when we were wrong promptly admitted it.

11. Sought through prayer and meditation to improve our conscious contact with God as we understood Him, praying only for knowledge of His will for us and the power to carry that out.

12. Having had a spiritual awakening as the result of these steps, we tried to carry this message to alcoholics and to practice these principles in all our affairs.

Not a religious organisation

Despite the references to "God" in the 12 Steps, it is important to realise that AA is not a religious organisation and has benefited many agnostics and atheists. Those who don't believe in God can instead see it as an acronym standing for Good Orderly Direction. They need only believe in a higher power which is greater than themselves – which could be simply the AA Group itself.

CASE STUDY: AA WORKS FOR ATHEIST

The difference between spending a Saturday night in Italy as opposed to in England is, according to former film star and Shakespearean actor John Fraser, "like going from heaven to hell".

John, who is aged 75, has been teetotal for 12 years and has lived on and off in Italy for the past forty years, during which time he has only ever seen a drunken Italian once.

He says, "Italians are appalled and bewildered at English drunkenness. To them being drunk in public is as unacceptable as evacuating your bowels in your underpants, whereas in England we are continually being shown scenes of young people unable to stand, vomiting in the gutter, strident and violent like inmates of a medieval madhouse."

"Knowing that civic and domestic violence is almost always alcohol related, the Government has extended the licensing hours in line with the Continent, making problem drinking much worse. There are no licensing laws in Italy because there is no drunkenness, not the other way around."

'Being an atheist, he is keen to dispel the myth that you need to believe in God to benefit from AA.'

A train journey between Rome and Milan after AC Milan had trounced Juventus in a high-profile soccer game proved particularly memorable in illustrating the contrast between the two cultures. Forty jubilant and rowdy fans raced along the corridors, banging doors and singing the anthems at the tops of their voices. But there wasn't a single can of beer to be found amongst them.

"They were certainly irritating to begin with" he recalls, "but a nice lady asked them to quieten down, and thereafter they were like mice. Italian mice are pretty noisy but they are not dangerous, whereas in England I've seen drink turn wonderful adorable people into Genghis Kahn."

John, who used to drink a minimum of a bottle of wine and two large whiskies virtually every night, defeated his drink problem by joining AA and did not require a medical detox.

> 'There is a popular theory that you have to hit rock bottom to stop drinking, but that's not true at all.'

Being an atheist, he is keen to dispel the myth that you need to believe in God to benefit from AA. He also hopes that his example can help to disprove another widely held misconception.

"There is a popular theory that you have to hit rock bottom to stop drinking, but that's not true at all" he explains. "You merely have to want to stop drinking more than you want to drink, and I wanted to stop because my partner was sick of me going to bed drunk every night. My friends were quite surprised as they didn't think that I needed to give up, but many of them have since admitted that I am now far less boring."

"Working at the AA switchboard used to act as a great way of strengthening my resolve because, although I could sometimes fool myself into thinking that my problem wasn't that bad, I realised that I didn't ever want to live the type of life that many of the incoming callers were living."

Not every teetotaller's cup of tea

The AA belief that those with drink problems suffer from a disease and that complete abstinence from alcohol represents the only solution can certainly be helpful for those with serious physical addictions, and for those who know others who suffer from them. It is not, on the other hand, necessarily helpful for someone with a mild psychological addiction to take the view that they have a disease, because this could encourage self-pity and prevent them from tackling potentially curable underlying problems that were causing them to drink in the first place. Nevertheless, they can certainly still benefit from the social interaction available from AA meetings during their period of initial sobriety.

> **"AA really does seem to suit some people very well, although not everyone likes the group approach or the idea of baring their soul in public."**
>
> **Prof. Ian Gilmore, President of The Royal College of Physicians**

Critics of AA tend to home in on the fact that it does not focus on what caused a drink problem in the first place, and that its philosophy prevents members from moving forward and putting their drink problems behind them. They observe, for example, that the organisation is notorious for members having relationships with each other, and that many members have merely swapped an obsession with alcohol for an obsession with AA. We would point out that an obsession with AA is an awful lot healthier than an obsession with alcohol and that these are very minor criticisms when seen in the context of the huge amount of good this organisation has done for millions of people worldwide.

Both SMART Recovery UK and SOS International offer those looking for a self-help group an alternative to the 12 Step approach

(See Appendix 3, pages 251 to 255 for details). Nevertheless, the vast majority of residential rehab clinics (See Chapter 5) actually use a 12 Step programme, based on the AA model but tweaked slightly to suit their own particular in-house style. They, and many others in the medical profession, also commonly advocate that their patients attend AA as an important part of their aftercare service.

> "Most major research over the last five to ten years shows 12 Step type abstinence has a higher rate of success of at least a few per cent over all other known methods of trying to be abstinent. But this certainly doesn't mean that abstinence can't be achieved by other means."
>
> Dr. Mike McPhillips, Consultant Psychiatrist and Lead Addiction Treatment Consultant at The Priory Hospital, Roehampton

Counselling

Once someone has become sober, counselling courses are often taken in conjunction with attending AA, and can play a valuable role in helping to tackle the underlying problems that caused excessive drinking. (See Case Study of Douglas Pendry, Chapter 4, page 91.)

Experts tend to stress that addiction counsellors are far more suitable than general counsellors, and that clinical psychologists, psychiatrists and psychotherapists are likely to prove next best. But, if none of these other options are available, general counsellors can still play a valuable role.

As long as someone has already become dry, one single hour-long counselling session a week could prove sufficient. However, if someone has yet to actually quit the drink, they are likely to require several sessions a week. Because addiction counsellors can cost anything between £40 and £150 an hour, paying privately could end up costing just as much as going to stay in a private residential rehab clinic.

> "I have come across hundreds of cases of people who are still drinking and seeing general counsellors once a fortnight or once a week for many months, but very few get into recovery. They really need to see a fully qualified addiction counsellor two or three times a week for at least six months."
>
> Keith Burns, Managing Director of independent advice and referral agency ADMIT Services

Even hypnosis should not be ruled out as a means of sorting out underlying problems, because some people have buried the root causes so deeply in their subconscious that no amount of conversation with the more conventional therapists will be able to get at them (See Appendix 3 for contact details of hypnotherapists).

In some cases, those who recover from psychological addictions and sort out their underlying problems may wish to try to return to drinking in moderation. In others, they are likely to take the view that they have been much happier as a teetotaller and that "if it ain't broke don't fix it".

CASE STUDY: HYPNOSIS DISCOVERS UNDERLYING CAUSE

Edmund Tirbutt, co-author of "Beat The Booze", finally identified one of the major causes of his psychological addiction to drink after being regressed to his childhood by a hypnotherapist. By this time, however, he had already been completely dry for five years.

Edmund, who is now 50, took the decision to become teetotal over 21 years ago after being ashamed at the depths to which his life had sunk. In the six years since leaving university he hadn't been able to attract a girlfriend or achieve a promotion at work, and friends had begun to desert him in droves. One of the few who remained warned him that he would never achieve anything unless he stopped drinking.

"That was sufficient to make me vow never to touch another drop" Edmund explains. "I just couldn't bear the thought of continuing to be a full-time loser whose only claim to fame was that he could be amusing when drunk. I remembered a schoolteacher who had advised 'If you need attention then do great things'. That became my new motto."

> 'If I hadn't managed to give up the drink first I would never have stuck with the hypnotherapy, which required considerable commitment.'

The sense of self-esteem gained by his new found sobriety gave him the courage to leave his job as a marketing assistant and follow his dream of being a freelance writer. The fact that his head was always clear gave him a vital edge in his work, and he was regularly commissioned by a range of magazines and had soon published two books. But this was merely the beginning of Edmund's journey.

After visiting London-based hypnotherapist Pauline Havelock-Searle for 12 sessions in 1993, he recalled how he had let down a school friend at the age of 10 by letting slip a highly personal secret he had been entrusted with. Being unable to live with the shame of his actions, he had buried the matter in his subconscious and had discussed it with no one since. This explained why he had often seemed to be his own worst enemy, as the guilt from his subconscious mind made him create obstacles to impede his progress.

Although he'd had no contact with the school friend concerned for 25 years, he managed to track him down and obtain his forgiveness. From then onwards Edmund's life improved out of all recognition. He wrote for 11 national newspapers, won the top awards in his field, married a wonderful partner and set up a successful copywriting company.

> 'I remembered a schoolteacher who had advised "If you need attention then do great things".'

He says, "If I hadn't managed to give up the drink first, I would never have stuck with the hypnotherapy, which required considerable commitment. Indeed, I had unsuccessfully tried a number of more conventional therapists first, but being dry gave me the self-confidence and determination to keep trying to find out what was causing my underlying unhappiness."

"Even though I am cured of my self-loathing, I will never touch another drop as my slightly obsessive personality also undoubtedly contributed to my drink problem, and I can't cure that. But I channel my energies into healthier pastimes like work and exercise instead."

Downing your sorrows

In some ways, giving up drinking is similar to dieting in that the longer you go on for the easier it becomes. But there will always be periods of disappointment in which the chances of relapses occurring become much higher than normal. So it is important to have a clearly defined strategy for coping with these, especially during the early months of giving up before the automatic pilot starts to take over.

> "We are all going to have a bad time in our lives. We are going to lose loved ones and jobs, and things are going to crash and burn. We will always wonder what it will be like and whether we will be brave enough and strong enough to cope."
>
> Joe Simpson, Mountaineer and Author (See Chapter 1, page 16)

However rosy the picture may appear at present, you can guarantee that it will not continue to be so indefinitely. Common setbacks that can cause relapses include relationship breakdowns – or even just fleeting rows with a partner – bereavements, job losses, being passed over for promotion, and property transactions falling through.

Don't let the problems ferment

It is essential that when these, or any other stressful scenarios, occur that the idea of having an alcoholic drink doesn't even enter your head, and this is why merely cutting down fails to work for so many people. When self-anaesthetising is still in the mindset as an option, it can all too easily start being called upon when the pain sets in. The primary weapon against such relapses is simply the knowledge that resorting to drink will make the problem worse not better.

> "Even if I learned I only had six months to live I would never drink again because I would want to enjoy those six months to the full."
>
> Thomas Page (See Case Study, page 42)

Can do attitude

One of the best ways of dealing with disappointment is turning a negative into a positive to create the foundations for future success, by using it to provide the motivation to go on to achieve bigger and better things. For example, if your partner leaves you, your response should be to find a far nicer one, and if you lose your job it should be seen as an opportunity to end up in a much better one. There is nothing quite like a setback to create an appetite for success, if you set about things with a positive frame of mind.

Another way of reducing your disappointment is simply to realise that there will always be many other people who are far worse off than yourself. Failing an exam or splitting up with a partner may seem like the end of the world at the time, but a trip around The Royal Marsden Hospital should soon make you realise how lucky you are.

Disappointment can also be reduced by being prepared to fully accept any part you may have played in contributing towards it. One of man's strongest urges is to be proved right all the time, but the ability to hold one's hands up and say "I was wrong" can remove a great deal of bitterness. After all, there isn't a person alive who hasn't made a mistake, so what's the big issue?

On the rocks

In the event of a divorce, for example, it is all too easy to take umbrage and reel off a list of unreasonable behaviours for which your estranged partner has been responsible. Even if you feel totally blameless for anything that happened within the marriage, you can't escape the fact that you agreed to get married in the first place. So, however unfortunate the outcome, you are at least partially to blame.

Strongly allied to this point is another home truth that can prevent us from getting badly hurt by things that other people say and do to us. Many people who hurt your feelings do so unintentionally as a result of misunderstandings, and even those who do so deliberately normally do it because they are unhappy themselves. This may be hard to accept, but it is true. So aiming to forgive them is likely to represent a much more productive way forward than seeking revenge.

Dealing with anxiety and depression

Anxiety and depression can also be major problems for those who are trying to give up alcohol completely, and can often be sufficient to necessitate medical attention in their own right – regardless of whether or not the sufferer has a serious drink problem.

Some people are naturally more anxious about potentially stressful situations than others, and may find that such anxiety attacks create an overwhelming desire to reach for the drink. In which case, they may well find that they have more success in giving up if they are regularly prescribed medication by a doctor to deal with the anxiety.

> "The vast majority of people I see have a dual diagnosis that is usually a substance misuse disorder and a neurotic mental health disorder such as anxiety, depression and phobias."
>
> Dr. Francis Keaney, Consultant Addiction Psychiatrist, National Addiction Centre, Institute of Psychiatry, King's College London

It may be necessary to be on anti-depressants or other prescribed medication for many years, or even permanently, to correct a chemical imbalance that you suffer from. But if this can help you overcome your drink problem it is surely a small price to pay? If taking a few pills regularly can restore your ability to cope to normal, why should you feel any more inadequate than someone who dyes their hair to correct a genetic predisposition to premature greyness?

For those with more normal anxiety levels who find themselves having to cope with one-off stressful situations, the Employee Assistance Programmes (EAPs) offered by many employers can offer useful free telephone and face-to-face counselling (See Chapter 9). Stress helplines available on some group and individual insurance policies can also prove valuable.

Dealing with relapse

But, as with learning to ride a bike, if you do fall off don't think twice about getting straight back on again. After all, if your car breaks down on a long journey, do you turn around and go back home again as soon as it is fixed? In most cases the idea will not even enter your head. You will be solely concerned with reaching your final destination. The same mentality should apply to giving up drinking.

CASE STUDY: A MYSTICAL EXPERIENCE

The story of 71-year-old Hugh Graham, who defeated his drink problem in 1979, defies virtually every rule of thumb spelt out by addiction experts.

Despite drinking one or two bottles of whisky a day, he was able to give up without a medical detox and, following a seven-year spell of being completely dry, he has managed to revert to moderate drinking without ever experiencing any cravings for alcohol. He drinks no more than two or three bottles of wine a month and enjoys the odd pint of beer.

Hugh took the decision to quit when his wife started talking about divorcing him shortly after his advertising and PR business had gone bust. The move, made after praying to the Christian God for help – which he didn't even believe in at the time – rescued his marriage and enabled him to establish himself as a photographer and author.

"You give up drinking when it's costing you more than money," he explains. "I'd been able to handle the disgrace and humiliation of my business failure and I'd even been able to come to terms with poor health and a steadily declining position in the community in which we lived, but I knew that I would never be able to handle life without my family. I loved and needed them too much."

> 'You give up drinking when it's costing you more than money.'

"I realise that the amount I was downing would have killed many people, and no one drinking even a fraction of what I was doing should consider giving up without medical help. I'm sure I was physically addicted, but there are inevitably those who argue that I wasn't because I had absolutely no withdrawal symptoms.

My own interpretation is simply that I was healed by a religious experience."

"I had been drinking heavily for 20 years and I couldn't function without drink before 10am and I used to have pins and needles all over my fingers and toes. But when I stopped, I reckon my mental capabilities improved every month for at least two years. I was also able to kick a 60-a-day smoking habit three years later, and the amount of money I saved from quitting both habits was enough to pay for both my kids to attend private school."

In the early stages of going dry, Hugh still went to pubs but drank apple juice, which many people obviously mistook for whisky. Rather than admit to having a drink problem, he invented a liver condition unrelated to drink and maintained that the medication his doctor had given for this could not be taken in conjunction with alcohol.

'When I stopped I reckon my mental capabilities improved every month for at least two years.'

After a couple of years, however, he came clean about his predicament and subsequently found himself spending a great deal of time talking to other people with drink problems.

"People who have a serious problem are attracted to those who are honest enough to admit having one and, having been given the gift of sobriety, I wanted to give something back by helping others. If you tell the whole unvarnished truth you can act as an inspirational example and as a support mechanism."

Key points

- You have a straight choice between acting now or spending the rest of your life worrying about it

- Once you have given up for a couple of years things should get a lot easier

- Don't be put off by those who are envious of your sobriety

- If you've had a physical addiction you should never touch another drop

- Pay due attention to diet and exercise during the early weeks and months

- Joining a self-help group can provide valuable social contact

- Experts stress that addiction counsellors are likely to be better than general counsellors

- Those who suffer from depression or anxiety attacks may need to take medication

Chapter 4:
Cutting Down

In some cases, cutting down alcohol consumption can simply be a lifestyle choice for people who never had a terribly serious drink problem in the first place. Whilst in others it can be essential to combat a psychological addiction. In both categories there are countless examples of those who lead happier and more fulfilled lives as a result of their efforts. But for a third category of drinker, namely those who have had physical addictions to alcohol, attempts to cut down virtually always fail.

It is human nature for people to suspect that they will be the one who reinvents the wheel, but it's no good thinking that it will merely be a question of mind over matter. The mind may be willing but the matter has changed. If you have had a physical addiction, your brain will have been permanently damaged.

"If someone has become physically addicted to alcohol their brain's reward centre is likely to have changed permanently in responsiveness to alcohol, so that if they pick up another drink they are likely to relapse to heavy drinking very quickly."

Dr. Bruce Trathen, Consultant Addiction Psychiatrist at DryOutNow.com

The grey area

In those rare cases of people who claim to have invented a system that allows them to drink again in moderation after giving up with the aid of a medical detox, it is highly likely that they never had a physical addiction in the first place. There is a huge grey area into which many problem drinkers fall, where it is not entirely clear whether their psychological addiction has also started to be accompanied by a physical addiction.

Different people have very different levels of tolerance to alcohol, and levels of consumption that could actually kill one person might not even cause a physical addiction in another after many years. Anyone who has the slightest doubt as to whether or not they have or have had a physical addiction should consult one or more of the numerous free or paid-for sources of professional help referred to in this book. Furthermore, even if they get the go-ahead from a doctor to test the water once again, they should clearly never touch another drop if they relapse to previous drinking levels.

Largely lifestyle

Many people who show little evidence of addiction decide to cut down their alcohol intake largely for lifestyle reasons. Whether the primary motivation behind such a move is to be more successful career-wise, healthier, better company or generally just happier, there can be no doubt that it works.

Surely this should be telling those with psychological addictions something? If someone can be much happier from giving up something that did not appear to pose a serious threat, then those who are seriously threatened should stand to benefit from a double win situation.

CASE STUDY: FINDING BETTER THINGS TO DO

29-year-old Claire Bannister admits that dramatically cutting down her alcohol intake happened "almost by mistake". Although a temporary move originally made whilst training for a marathon in January 2006, it soon became permanent.

"I felt so healthy that I've never really wanted to drink much again," she says. "I was still socialising in bars just as much but felt a lot happier and always seemed to have more money. Even two glasses of wine used to make me so lethargic that I would never want to do anything more during the rest of the evening other than eat dinner and watch TV."

"But now I play netball, see shows, visit friends, and have even taken up pole dancing lessons. Because my psychology has changed I now very rarely feel like a drink, and when I do it is usually because there's something lovely available like a good champagne. A major problem with our society is that we have been conditioned to feel that we can't have a good time without having a drink, which is so clearly untrue."

> 'I felt so healthy that I've never really wanted to drink much again.'

Claire emphasises that an alcohol-free Muslim wedding she attended in India in December 2004 was the best wedding she's ever been to "by an absolute mile". Guests chatted excitedly, played games and pranks on each other, ate lovely food, danced and enjoyed the music.

"In India they have far less inhibitions and are more comfortable in themselves, and as soon as the music starts they fall over each other to get on the dance floor" she recalls. "In England, on the other hand, I've noticed that people like to have a drink before they start dancing. The dance floor is normally fairly empty to begin with, then people start becoming very silly."

But she stresses that she tries hard not to preach about the fact that she rarely drinks alcohol. Indeed, she hardly ever mentions the subject, usually brushing off those who enquire why she's sipping a soft drink with excuses like it's because she is driving, making an early start or pacing herself after drinking earlier. This rarely causes any eyebrows to be raised in her job in banking, which involves a lot of client entertaining, but she sometimes finds people raising the subject socially.

> 'We have been conditioned to feel that we can't have a good time without having a drink, which is so clearly untrue.'

"The reason that I often play it down and make excuses is that it's easier on other people, because many of them are sensitive about their drinking habits and can think you are being judgemental if you start blowing your own trumpet," Claire explains. "The really hardened drinkers often try and persuade me to have a drink, but it's so obvious that they are subconsciously trying to drag me down to their level in order to try and justify their own habits."

"But when I do actually come clean with people about the fact that I'm hardly drinking any more, they often end up regarding me as a bit of a role model and cut down their own drinking hugely as a result."

Psychological addiction

Many people who only ever suffered from a psychological addiction never actually want to drink again once they have managed a significant dry spell. They realise they are much healthier, happier and more productive, and the very fact that they are teetotal has given them a completely new sense of self-worth and provided a platform upon which to rebuild their life. Every time they come across a situation in which other people are drinking it makes them feel a few inches taller because they are reminded of the immensity of their achievement.

They are probably enjoying the benefits of excelling in the workplace and of having far more success with the opposite sex than they used to. They may even be in a stable relationship with a partner who has nothing but admiration for their ability to triumph in the face of adversity. So why change a winning formula?

> "There are two main symptoms of psychological addiction. Stereo-typed patterns of drinking at the same time each day and when drink starts taking priority over other things."
>
> Dr. Bruce Trathen, Consultant Addiction Psychiatrist at DryOutNow.com

Never touching another drop can therefore be especially effective for those who formerly suffered from low self-esteem. Simply cutting down does not provide the same sense of individuality and achievement when alcohol is present. Indeed, the person concerned may well yearn for a drink in the same way that someone on a diet is likely to crave cream cakes when they attend a tea party.

Those who simply cut down are also unable to benefit from the automatic pilot that teetotallers typically find takes over somewhere between one and two years after going dry. Although the mind can sometimes adapt to follow sets of rules that become habit forming, the process is much more complicated than simply adapting to one rule that has no exceptions or grey areas.

Methods of cutting down

But those with psychological addictions who simply cannot envisage going without alcohol altogether can sometimes manage to cut down successfully if they impose the very highest standards of self-discipline once they have tackled their underlying problems. Any method of cutting down that could work for you should not be ruled out, and problem drinkers have proved most ingenious in coming up with their own systems.

'The only statistic we care about is you. Whatever percentages of others have succeeded or failed to control their drinking is of no relevance.'

Nevertheless, we have devised our own "12 Strides For Cutting Down", based on methods used by drinkers who have successfully managed to keep their drinking under control. If you cannot think of a suitable strategy yourself, then try using several of the Strides shown opposite.

12 STRIDES FOR CUTTING DOWN

1. Replace time spent drinking with exercise, and benefit from the more natural feeling of well-being created by the release of the body's own chemicals. (See Case Study of Ted Nye, page 82.)

2. Find new hobbies and interests to occupy the time you would otherwise spend drinking. (See Case Study of Douglas Pendry, page 91.)

3. Never drink on your own or when you are in a bad mood or feeling depressed or anxious.

4. Limit drinking to weekends, holidays or "special occasions", or insist on having two or three alcohol-free days every week.

5. Try to introduce other changes of habit so that you become less resistant to the idea of changing your routine, i.e. changing the newspaper you read, getting rid of the television, getting up an hour earlier or switching your evening meal to a brief snack at 6pm.

6. Take up drinking some of the newer and more realistic alcohol substitutes (See pages 87 and 88).

7. Keep a drink diary to accurately record your drinking habits. (See Case Study of Rebecca Sampson, page 85.)

8. Dilute your alcohol intake by switching to weaker drinks or alternating any alcoholic drink you have with a soft drink.

9. Avoid drinking in rounds, because it means you will end up drinking as fast as the fastest drinker.

10. Decide how much you are going to drink before you go out, and stick to it.

11. Take less money with you when you go out and leave the credit cards at home.

12. If you know that seeing certain people always involves drinking a lot, try to see less of them.

Also worthy of consideration is an online self-help programme offered by Moderation Management to help people cut down their alcohol consumption (See Appendix 3, page 253) and a pioneering form of treatment that connects a problem drinker's brain activity to specialist video games (See below).

GOING BEYOND THE CONVENTIONAL WITH MODERN SCIENCE

An innovative scientific technique that utilises highly specialist video games boasts an unusually high success rate for curing drink problems (See Appendix 3, page 263). It claims to enable people to eventually drink alcohol again in moderation by repairing damaged brain functions.

The technique is available privately and – in certain circumstances – via the NHS, but regular attendance is required at clinics in either West London or St. Albans. Electrodes are placed on the patient's scalp to detect the area of their brain that is malfunctioning and causing the compulsion to drink. The signals are then analysed and the imbalances are tackled by connecting the patient's brain activity to a video game.

> 'People usually drink because they have a brainwave band which is under-functioning, and it makes them feel agitated.'

The idea is to get the brain to influence the video game in a positive way, so that the patient becomes trained to think like someone who doesn't have a drink problem. This requires considerable application between hour-long treatment sessions, which will typically take place twice a week for at least three months – very severe cases may, on the other hand, require six or nine months.

Dr. Surinder Kaur, who has pioneered the treatment, says "Whenever patients have a craving they will see the video game change in front of their eyes and will learn how to get the game moving again and make the craving go away. Outside the sessions they can get rid of the cravings by imagining the video game and applying the same techniques that they use during treatment to get the game moving again."

The treatment sessions also use another, different kind of specialist video game to raise the feelgood factor within the patient's brain so that they never feel the need to create artificial highs by having a drink.

"People usually drink because they have a brainwave band which is under-functioning, and it makes them feel agitated" continues Dr. Kaur. "That calm, happy, contented feeling is normally in short supply with anyone with addiction problems. We are effectively giving the individual the power to self-regulate their behaviour, but we avoid the potential downsides of many other treatments. Attending some self-help groups and counselling sessions can actually make you feel worse because you are talking about a problem that is depressing without necessarily seeing any possible solution."

> 'That calm, happy, contented feeling is normally in short supply with anyone with addiction problems.'

Even those who find it impractical to get to West London or St. Albans twice a week because they don't live somewhere nearby, may be able to arrange more intensive courses that involve attending treatment every day for one or two months – if they arrange their own local accommodation.

Breaking the rules

Being permanently teetotal is clearly a better solution than cutting down for those who lack self-discipline because, whilst imposing rules is all very well, sticking to them is a different matter. Most people who aim to cut down therefore inevitably end up drinking far more than they originally intended.

If you decide to drink only at weekends, the weekend will probably start off beginning on Friday night and ending on Saturday night in order to ensure that your drinking isn't allowed to affect your performance at work. But it doesn't take long before it starts on Friday lunchtime, and then possibly even Thursday evening!

Similarly, those who allow themselves a "hair of the dog" on Sunday morning will find that it soon turns into a whole dog, and one with a vicious bite! Before long, Sunday lunchtime will also be allowed and the levels consumed will probably be sufficient to cause a hangover on the Monday morning.

> "Cutting down is still better than doing nothing at all, even if you are sometimes still drinking too much. What is important is that the total volume is not too excessive."
>
> Alison Rogers, Chief Executive of the British Liver Trust

Those who decide that they are only going to drink on holiday can soon find that their definition of a holiday becomes terribly flexible. Once it is allowed to include merely long weekends, it often results in the drinker actually making a point of booking as many Mondays off work as possible in order to maximise their exposure to long weekends of heavy drinking.

Even those who never break the rule they set themselves of never drinking on their own may well find that they spend very little time on their own, and that all sorts of people they have little in common with suddenly start being invited round for a drink! Where has that got them?

Some can manage it

Not everyone lacks self-discipline, however, and not everyone suffered from low self-esteem in the first place. They may have had other issues that they have managed to successfully address through a significant dry spell.

> 'The term drink problem, like cancer, refers to literally hundreds of different conditions and each one has their own causes and individual solutions.'

Those who have the close support of a partner and family who are able to monitor their behaviour are also more likely to be able to revert to drinking in moderation than those who live in isolation – although living on your own is clearly more conducive to cutting down than living with others who actually encourage drinking to excess.

CASE STUDY: WINNING A RUNNING BATTLE

Ted Nye describes running as his "new bottle". The 45-year-old journalist realised that the only realistic way for someone with his type of "all or nothing personality" to get his drinking under control was to become obsessed with a healthier pastime.

Although it took a while to get fit when he made the change nine years ago, he managed to convert himself from a slouch to a good club runner who goes for a serious jog at least five times a week. The move has completely transformed his life and made a huge difference to his physical appearance.

> 'Defeating his drink problem has required considerable mental resolve in addition to his new found passion for running.'

He says "I found running both liberating and therapeutic. It gave me time out from the pressures of work to think, and the resulting weight loss was uplifting, with many people observing that I had transformed myself from an ugly duckling into a prince charming. Working on a national newspaper involved being bombarded with offers of lunch and dinner, and my weight had ballooned with the horrible descent into binging that accompanied these."

"The problem had also been greatly exacerbated by the arrival of my first child in 1990. Although the birth was a thrill, it also resulted in breaking the robust bond that I'd previously enjoyed with my wife. The love formerly given to me was transferred to our newborn, a process accentuated by the arrival of two further children during the next three years. From being the only recipient of my wife's love, I had become one of four vying for it. Selfishly, I turned to drink."

Initially, Ted gave up drinking altogether for 13 months but, because he had a psychological as opposed to a physical addiction, he did not need a medical detox. For the past eight years he has allowed himself to drink occasionally but is proud "to have the beast under control".

Ted doesn't drink at home and can go for weeks without alcohol, but he does drink on a social basis with people he truly likes and enjoys being with. He even permits himself the odd binge, but it is always followed by a period of not drinking at all.

> 'The move has completely transformed his life and made a huge difference to his physical appearance.'

Although he was never tempted to turn to AA or other support groups for help, he admits that defeating his drink problem has required considerable mental resolve in addition to his new found passion for running.

"The clincher for me was the prospect of not seeing my kids grow up and not being able to play football with them because of my drink-induced poor health, but it still required immense willpower, and the ability to say 'no' was paramount."

"I had a reputation as a drinker and many people liked to dine with me because they knew they were in for a good time," he continues, "so breaking out of this vicious circle was difficult. Suddenly people who I thought were friends disappeared into the distance."

Zero tolerance

For every example of unmitigated success in cutting down like Ted Nye, there are hundreds of others who fail to stick to the rules they have imposed. The chances are that if someone has broken those rules once it will become a recurring theme.

It's all very well saying it only happened because I had this problem or that problem, but life is all about having problems, and if your regime couldn't cope with one issue why should you expect it to cope with another one in the future?

A classic mistake is for someone to begin a new romance and to assume that, because everything seems rosy at the time, they will never have any further setbacks. But even the most rock solid relationships will involve the occasional spat sufficient to make the idea of self-anaesthetising attractive if it is still lingering in the mindset. If you meet anyone who insists that they have never had a cross word with their husband or wife, they are either the biggest liar on earth or they have been married little more than five minutes.

> 'If you have a drink problem you have a straight choice between doing something about it now or spending the rest of your life worrying about it. There is no middle ground.'

Those who have genuinely conquered their problem will feel no more anxiety when holding an alcoholic drink in their hand than they would when holding a cup of tea or coffee. If you don't operate with this level of confidence it is probably time to give up altogether.

Cutting down without stopping

We cannot repeat often enough the message that we strongly recommend anyone with a drink problem to stop the rot by giving up alcohol completely for a significant initial period in order to maximise their chances of addressing the underlying issues.

'When a fireman is confronted with a fire, he doesn't spend the first few hours trying to work out what has caused it.'

But there are many cases of people who will simply not entertain doing this, and if they can at least reduce their alcohol intake to less dangerous levels, they will clearly be better off than if they take no action at all. As demonstrated by the case study of Rebecca Sampson below, keeping a drink diary and changing a few long-standing habits can help greatly.

CASE STUDY: CUTTING DOWN WITH THE DRINK DIARY

Having become concerned at drinking one and a half bottles of red wine every evening, Rebecca Sampson finally summoned the courage to phone Drinkline in January 2007.

"My husband had become concerned about my behaviour, because I had become argumentative and restless," she recalls, "and I was particularly concerned that the alcohol was interfering with my relationship with my seven year-old son, as it was stopping me helping him with his homework and doing all the other 'childreny' things like reading him stories."

"I just couldn't wait for him to get to bed so that I could start my drinking but, now I've cut down, I'm actually enjoying being with him again and I'm far better tempered, happier and more positive."

'Being at home all the time and not using my brain made me feel a bit worthless and created resentment.'

Drinkline referred Rebecca to KCA, her local social services funded community drug and alcohol centre based in Ashford in Kent (See Appendix 3, page 248), where she attended 12 weekly counselling and harm reduction sessions.

By the end she had cut down her evening's drinking to a bottle of wine, which means she no longer suffers from serious hangovers, and she has managed to have two evenings every week without any alcohol at all. Eventually, she hopes to only drink at weekends.

The harm reduction sessions proved particularly useful for practical tips. For example, Rebecca had always started drinking at 6pm and had sat on the same chair. At first she moved the start time back to 7pm and by week five she was not starting until 9pm – after her son was in bed. She has also made a point of drinking from smaller glasses, leaving lengthy gaps between opening the wine bottle and actually starting drinking, and drinking in different chairs.

Keeping a drink diary was an integral part of the process. In it she recorded the day, time, and place of any drinking, together with details of who she was drinking with, what and how much she was drinking, and how she felt both before and after drinking. She would then discuss her entries at her harm reduction sessions and review how she was changing her habit.

'I just couldn't wait for him to get to bed so that I could start my drinking, but I'm actually enjoying being with him again.'

"The drink diary helps you see the progress you are making and makes you aware of your reward systems" she explains. "The harm reduction specialist makes you realise that it's not a good idea to reward yourself with a drink and suggests replacing it with something else, like having a hot bubble bath with candles or buying an item of clothing or a CD."

"In addition to harm reduction, the counselling sessions managed to get to the bottom of why I was drinking. Being at home all the time and not using my brain had made me feel a bit worthless and created resentment, so I am trying to find a stimulating job which will make me feel more valued. It's really great to have someone objective to listen to, because your friends don't always want to tell you the truth in case they disappoint you."

Drinking alcohol substitutes

Whether you are simply trying to drink less or are attempting to return to drinking in moderation after giving up for an initial period and sorting out the underlying causes of a psychological addiction, there is an important new tool available to you that wasn't generally available a few years ago.

It is now possible to obtain de-alcoholised beer and wine that tastes much more realistic than the artificial wines and beers that have been sold for decades in supermarkets. Both The Alcohol-Free Shop, founded in 2006, and The LoNo Drinks Company, founded in 2002, now provide a wide range of highly effective substitutes.

"We found the alcohol-free range in the shops had barely changed in 30 years. It was still basically Kaliber lager and Eisberg wine. We found Becks alcohol-free and a couple of white and sparkling wines in Sainsbury's, Tesco and Asda, but that was about it."

John Risby, Co-founder, The Alcohol-Free Shop

The UK has certainly lagged behind other countries in this respect. In Sweden, for example, restaurants are legally obliged to include an alcohol-free wine on the wine list, and as long ago as 1986, Ariel wines became recognised in the international wine world when the judges in Los Angeles selected Ariel Blanc for the Gold Award in a blind taste test against wines containing alcohol.

Any wine buff will naturally be sceptical, but before anyone turns their noses up at the idea that anything could pass off as the real thing, we suggest that they at least give this innovation a try. Full details of what is available can be found on the companies' respective websites.

Where to buy de-alcoholised wines and beers

- The Alcohol-Free Shop – www.alcoholfree.co.uk (Wine, beer and other alcohol-free products)

- The LoNo Drinks Company – www.lono.co.uk (Comprehensive selection of wines and aperitifs)

(For more detailed information on both organisations see Appendix 3, pages 274 and 276.)

These alcohol substitutes are proving particularly popular with pregnant women and others giving up drink altogether for a period of time, as well as with drivers, weight watchers, and those who want to avoid alcohol for religious or cultural reasons. They also appeal to people who want to limit their alcohol intake but still enjoy a genuine beer or glass of wine at social gatherings. Many drink these substitutes during the week and let their hair down at weekends.

> "It's extraordinary the amount of times the host and hostess haven't told them it's de-alcoholised and no-one notices. We've had thousands of blind tastings at shows and no more than a handful of people have ever spotted that it's not normal wine."
>
> Dale Hemming-Tayler, Managing Director of The LoNo Drinks Company

These substitute wines – and in some cases the beers – are exactly the same as their normal counterparts all the way through to the bottling stage, when the alcohol is then removed. This means that the flavour and all the original characteristics remain but the drink has only between one third and one half of the calories of the real thing – therefore providing a valuable additional lifestyle benefit!

Because all the anti-oxidants and other goodness remain, these substitutes are just as effective as alcoholic drinks in combating heart disease amongst very moderate middle-aged and older drinkers (See Chapter 2, page 24). Indeed there is even some evidence emerging to suggest that non-alcoholic beer can help to combat cancer.

> "I think some of the non-alcoholic substitutes are fantastic, particularly the red wines. The red grape skin has an anti-oxidant effect and the sugar and fermentation process helps you glow. Non-alcoholic Cobra beer is also very good and makes you glow. You couldn't be under the influence of alcohol from these drinks, however much you drank."
>
> Dr. Surinder Kaur, Addiction Specialist, The Hale Clinic, London

Although these types of drinks are effectively "alcohol-free" and are recognised as such by other European countries, they are, through some strange quirk of the law in this country, not actually allowed to be called that – as the title is only permissible for drinks with an alcohol content that does not exceed 0.05% abv (alcohol by volume). So, under UK law, they are officially referred to as "de-alcoholised" drinks.

All de-alcoholised drinks have an alcohol content of below 0.5% abv. This means they are safe for a teetotaller to drink, containing no more alcohol than some soft drinks sold in supermarkets. You would need to drink 120 bottles of them in one hour to equate with drinking a bottle of alcoholic wine! Anyone on medication who has been advised to avoid alcohol should, however, first check with their doctor before trying these drinks.

> "I had to be dry for several years from 1997 after picking up a parasite infection, and it was very hard to find anything enjoyable to drink. I ended up having to drink glass after glass of sparkling water, so I certainly sympathise with those going on the wagon."
>
> **Esther Rantzen, Founder of ChildLine**

Anyone who really can't tell the difference between de-alcoholised substitutes and the real thing clearly can't justify drinking alcohol any longer simply by the phrases "I just enjoy the taste" or "Wine is good for the heart".

Yet someone with an addiction to alcohol clearly has a vested interest in finding the taste of de-alcoholised drinks to be inferior, so there is a lot to be said for ensuring that your first tasting is a completely blind one – by getting someone else to pour out real wine in one glass and de-alcoholised wine in another, without telling you which is which.

Even those with pallets sophisticated enough to spot the difference should bear in mind that, just as alcohol is an acquired taste that can take time to get used to, it can take some people time to adjust to de-alcoholised drinks. If it was worth learning to love alcohol then surely it must be worth learning to love de-alcoholised?

CASE STUDY: GETTING TO THE BOTTOM OF THINGS

"It can take half a lifetime to reach that point of self-awareness when you realise that you have to put your life in order, and you may have to experience terrible depths of misery first" explains 80-year-old Douglas Pendry. "But if you can get to the bottom of it all and make sense of why things have happened, you can regain control."

An unexpected divorce and 20 years of doing a job in advertising surrounded by "awful people telling lies" saw him reach a point when alcohol had become his best friend and he couldn't stand getting out of bed every morning.

> 'If you can get to the bottom of it all and make sense of why things have happened, you can regain control.'

An initial attempt to beat his psychological addiction in 1986, saw him falling off the wagon after going dry for a year because, although he demonstrated plenty of willpower, he had failed to fully address the underlying issues that had driven him to drink in the first place. But a second attempt a year later, after having half a dozen sessions with an NHS psychologist, enabled him to completely turn his life around.

He stresses, however, that it was only his sheer persistence and refusal to take 'no' for an answer that ensured he eventually received the necessary access to the psychologist, therefore reinforcing our message that those who shout loudest tend to end up being the primary beneficiaries of State-funded treatment (See Chapter 5).

"Talking to the psychologist enabled me to wrap up all the bad things in a bag and throw them on a bonfire" he explains. "There were anxieties created by my childhood that I simply hadn't been aware of through self-analysis. I was, for example, brought up by a divorced mother who was exceptionally possessive, and during wartime I didn't even see much of her because I had to live with an aunt and uncle in the country."

"But I had to shout and scream at the local health authority to be allowed to see the psychologist in the first place. The doctors I had originally seen had merely wanted to prescribe drugs, which weren't doing me any good, so during a period of contemplation in a chapel I realised that I was simply going to have to help myself by making a noise."

> 'Talking to the psychologist enabled me to wrap up all the bad things in a bag and throw them on a bonfire.'

Whilst initially going totally dry, Douglas was able to settle in a completely different line of work in a low-pressure administrative capacity, which made him much happier. He also took up sculpture, which occupied most of the time that he used to spend drinking. After a year, he therefore felt able to resume a much more moderate relationship with alcohol.

Once again, we see the importance of going dry for an initial period to stop the rot and ensuring that you have the maximum possible chance of addressing the underlying problems and effecting necessary lifestyle changes.

Key points

- If you have suffered a physical addiction you should never touch another drop

- Anyone who is unsure if they have a physical addiction should seek advice

- Cutting down does not provide the same sense of achievement when alcohol is present as giving up

- Cutting down does not enable you to benefit from an automatic pilot as when giving up

- Those who want to cut down should give up for an initial period

- But if they can't, simply reducing the amount they drink is better than taking no action at all

- Give the better de-alcoholised substitutes a try

- Those who cut down often drink more than the government's recommended safe-drinking guidelines

Chapter 5:
Getting Professional Help

Whether you are able to obtain professional help free of charge to combat your drink problem is likely to depend both on the area you live in and on the extent to which you are prepared to push and make your voice heard.

State-funded facilities for alcohol treatment can vary markedly from one postcode to the next, and the expertise and attitudes of GPs can also differ significantly. Many GPs will have great contacts with local community alcohol treatment services and an in-depth knowledge of alcohol-related issues, but some may be less conversant with the options available and have little experience of dealing with drink problems.

> "In some cases we have been informed by service users that GPs may have negative attitudes towards them and a reluctance to provide specialist support, and we have identified a need for training to encourage GPs to work with clients with alcohol and mental health needs. In some cases, individuals may be diagnosed as depressed without providing support for an additional alcohol problem."
>
> **Richard Kramer, Director of Policy at Turning Point**

It is therefore important to realise that you are quite entitled to transfer to another GP, either in the same practice or elsewhere, without giving a reason. But even the most sympathetic and knowledgeable GP can be handicapped by poor local State-funded facilities, and an essential message to take on board is that those who shout the loudest often get the best results from the system.

In the case study of Douglas Pendry (See Chapter 4, page 91), for example, we see how someone's refusal to take 'no' for an answer finally secured access to an NHS psychologist who enabled him to "wrap up all the bad things in a bag and throw them on a bonfire".

> **"If my GP wouldn't refer me I would change my GP and if the NHS says it has a big waiting list I would kick and scream until I received the appropriate treatment."**
>
> **Prof. Griffith Edwards, Emeritus Professor of Addiction Behaviour at the National Addiction Centre, Institute of Psychiatry, King's College London**

Even those with access to little or no State-funded help in their locality may still find they are able to secure free treatment in another part of the country through an alcohol-related charity or via State-funded entry to a private residential rehabilitation clinic.

PRIVATE REHAB ON THE STATE

Broadway Lodge, a residential rehabilitation clinic based in Weston-super-Mare in Somerset, uses a combination of motivational techniques and the 12 Step approach to help those with drink problems and other addictions.

As all the problem drinkers it treats have had serious physical addictions, they are taught that they have been suffering from a disease, which can only be cured by abstinence. Whilst this doesn't mean they are not 'accountable' for the consequences of their previous behaviour, it does mean that they should not feel 'responsible' for them.

"It's about dealing with the addiction and not with the substance," explains Peter Smith, Head of Counselling at Broadway Lodge. "The problem is their addictive nature, so we need to look at their behavioural psychological profile and change the way that they deal with problems. A lot of people initially only come in here to get their families off their backs but, once they've done a couple of weeks, they begin to feel a lot better physically and start to want to complete the recovery for themselves."

> 'It's about dealing with the addiction and not with the substance.'

"The first step is to get them to realise that they have a problem, and to share experiences in groups about their drinking and its consequences. Then they need to accept that they need help," he continues. "By being here they realise they are not the only ones with a problem, so breaking the isolation is very important and the real power of this place lies in the coffee lounge."

Patients entering Primary Care, which lasts around eight weeks, are assigned domestic responsibilities such as helping to prepare the dining room for meals, and are subdivided into three groups. They are not allowed to watch television or listen to the radio during their stay – although they are allowed to read newspapers. One especially stressful and painful activity they have to undertake is to write their life history during the second week and read it to their group. Around two thirds complete the whole course.

Many of them then move onto Secondary Care, which lasts for 13 weeks and has a similar completion rate. It is less structured than Primary Care and patients have to do their own shopping and cooking.

'Breaking the isolation is very important and the real power of this place lies in the coffee lounge.'

During 2007, Primary Care cost £1,512 a week and Secondary Care £566 a week. Fees, however, are not an issue for around three quarters of patients because they are State funded. Most patients are referred by social services after unsuccessfully trying local non-residential addiction services, but problem drinkers who contact Broadway Lodge directly will be pointed in the right direction with regard to trying to find State funding – although the application process is likely to take several months.

Being a registered charity, Broadway Lodge can, in some circumstances, also pay for patients out of its own funds, but it will not do so until they have tried all other methods of getting the necessary funding and have tried to help themselves by attending non-residential treatment centres.

Further information about Broadway Lodge and contact details are available in Appendix 3 (page 228).

Free advice from private organisations

It can also be possible to obtain a great deal of initial free advice from the private sector. Some of the specialist intermediary services detailed on page 112 will provide callers with free advice up to a certain level over the phone, and The Priory Group offers free confidential no obligation, face-to-face assessments to alcohol-dependent people or their close relatives and friends. These will include discussion of your drinking history, lifestyle and different treatment options.

Paying for private advice

Those who experience problems in obtaining free treatment still have the option of paying privately for either residential or non-residential care. Six weeks in many reputable UK private residential rehab clinics may cost in the region of £5,000 to £12,000, and those prepared to travel to South Africa can pay nearer £3,000 (See Case Study of Nigel Cockburn, page 114).

These sums may appear frightening at first glance, but should be within reach for those with equity in their own home. Bearing in mind what you might lose if you don't get the problem sorted, borrowing could be worth considering. Alternatively, you could look at whether family members are able to help.

"The prices involved are nothing in comparison to what a divorce or losing a job is likely to cost, and it does not normally take long for someone with a serious drink problem to find themselves facing one of these situations."

David Gilmour, Co-founder of specialist intermediary Re-cover

---

Off-the-record treatment

The fact that private treatment, both residential and non-residential, can be accessed without introduction from your GP means that your drink problem need not appear on your medical records. But many experts argue that, if you are in a bad state, what appears on your medical records should be the least of your worries and, as discussed in Chapter 3, many GPs can make an immensely valuable contribution to the recovery process. So cutting them out of the loop could prove counterproductive.

But there will always be certain problem drinkers who don't want their GP to know about their condition. They may, for example, mix with their GP socially or work in a field in which being known to have a drink problem could significantly impair their progress.

Whether a GP reveals this aspect of your past to a potential employer is likely to depend both on the attitude of the GP concerned and the type of job. Although some employers are enlightened enough to realise that those who have conquered drink problems make better than average employees (see Chapter 9, pages 192-193), others will be extremely wary.

Driving licence

Some people may also fear that involving their GP could cost them their driving licence. If you have a drink problem it's up to you to tell the Driver and Vehicle Licensing Agency (DVLA) but, because this may result in losing your driving licence for a period of time, most problem drinkers don't.

Your GP is not obliged to contact the DVLA about your drink problem, but they may do so if they feel it is necessary. A friend or family member may also report you to the DVLA, and this could result in a medical investigation, which would probably start with the DVLA contacting your GP.

Insurance

Having a drink problem on your records can also affect your chances of being eligible to take out life assurance and certain types of health insurance or, if you are accepted, it can greatly increase the cost. But this is only likely to be a problem in the early years of recovery and, as long as you never touch another drop, your eligibility for insurance will gradually improve until you are eventually accepted under standard terms.

Additionally, those who shield their problem from their GP and fail to declare it on their insurance application should be aware that their insurer can refuse to pay out at the claims stage if it subsequently finds out. Sometimes, for example, policyholders mention something about their drinking habits when undergoing a fairly minor operation on the NHS, and this finds its way into their medical records and subsequently disqualifies them from having an insurance claim paid.

> "Never let considerations towards insurance prevent you getting medical help. Premiums will be loaded for a period after going dry, but the longer you go on for the less it usually costs. Eventually you can draw a line under the past."
>
> Matt Rann, Head of Underwriting and Claims at AEGON Scottish Equitable

When you take out life or health cover, insurers will assess the extent to which your stated alcohol intake – along with any co-existing depression or other health problems – increases the likelihood of you making a claim on your policy. If they are concerned by the information provided on your application form, they are likely to require you to have a medical examination with an independent doctor in your area. This will involve, amongst other things, undergoing liver function tests.

If you are applying for a life assurance policy, you are unlikely to be granted cover if you currently have a serious drink problem. If, however, you then give up alcohol altogether and reapply, you are likely to be accepted once you have been completely dry for two years – or possibly even one year – if medical reports confirm there is little risk of relapse.

Someone who has been dry for only a couple of years may have to pay four times the standard premium, but by the time they have managed five years they may not have to pay any premium loading at all. You are, on the other hand, likely to have to be completely dry for 10 years, or possibly even 15 years, before you are accepted at standard premium rates for either critical illness cover, which pays out a tax-free lump sum if you are diagnosed with one of a stated number of critical conditions, or income protection insurance, which pays out a regular tax-free income if you are unable to work as a result of long-term sickness or disability.

Private treatment and medical records

Even if you approach a private residential rehab clinic directly, it is likely to ask your permission to write to your GP to obtain a copy of your medical history – to check there aren't any conditions you have forgotten to mention that could cause complications during its treatment processes. The key point to take on board is that simply obtaining a medical history from your GP should not result in your drink problem being entered on your medical records, as long as you haven't discussed your drink problem with the GP.

As far as your GP need be concerned, you could be at the clinic for numerous others reasons, such as receiving treatment for depression or merely taking a therapeutic break, and the clinic should word the request for your medical history in a way that doesn't explicitly give anything away.

> "If you go to a clinic or addiction counsellor recommended by us it doesn't go on your medical records. The clinic merely asks your permission to apply for a recent medical history, and your GP can't write down anything about your drinking unless you actually volunteer that information to the GP."
>
> Keith Burns, Managing Director of independent advice and referral agency ADMIT Services

The same principle should also apply with non-residential private treatment, such as counselling or medical detox services. But, if you are determined to keep your drink problem off your medical records and fail to receive the necessary assurances from the treatment providers, the surest way of avoiding anxiety is simply to refuse to allow them to contact your GP at all.

Private medical insurance

You may, however, have a problem with keeping your treatment off your medical records if you wish to pay for it via private medical insurance (PMI) – which enables you to jump the NHS queue and enjoy the comfort of a private room. This is because PMI providers will only cover treatment for conditions that are verified by your GP.

Very few PMI providers, in fact, cover treatment for alcohol-related conditions, but some will cover depression under certain types of policy, and drink problems and depression often go hand in hand. As long as the insurer doesn't know that alcohol is involved, it may be prepared to fund your residential rehab treatment on the grounds that you need treatment for a depressive illness.

But there is a very fine ethical line to be trodden here and the key is to get the clinic to deal with the paperwork connected with the claim. If it is prepared to say that you are being treated for depression then you have done nothing wrong.

State-funded treatment and medical records

In theory, you also have a right to keep your drink problem off your medical records if you receive treatment from a State-funded service that does not require initial GP referral.

"In the NHS, confidentiality should be respected in the same way as in the independent sector. You have an absolute right to confidentiality with very few exceptions. Such exceptions might include a direct risk of harm to yourself or others or a significant risk to a child in your care. By contrast, there are comparatively few situations in which you would be at serious medical risk through insisting that your doctor does not disclose a past history of addiction to colleagues."

Dr. Mike McPhillips, Consultant Psychiatrist and Lead Addiction Treatment Consultant at The Priory Hospital, Roehampton

In practice, however, it is not as easy to keep information off your medical records when undergoing State-funded treatment as it is when paying for private treatment. Those who work for the NHS and social services tend to take a far more paternalistic attitude, and may phrase requests for medical histories in a way which is far more explicit. They could also make your treatment a less urgent priority if you refuse them permission to contact your GP.

But, once again, it should be stressed that involving a helpful and knowledgeable GP will, in many cases, do a lot more good than harm. For most people, the primary concern should be to get better rather than to worry about the potential consequences of having a drink problem on their medical records a few years' later. There's not much point in having an unblemished medical record if your brain is too addled to hold down a job!

What's actually available on the State?

The State-funded alcohol addiction treatment facilities that are available in your area are likely to subdivide between those funded by the NHS and those funded by social services. The distinction between the two is not always terribly obvious or, indeed – from the end user's point of view – terribly important.

There is actually a huge amount of overlap between both camps, and in some areas they even operate from the same building. There can also be a further overlap with charities and voluntary organisations, so it is actually possible to receive free treatment funded by several different sources.

Local community alcohol services, sometimes known as Community Alcohol Teams (CATs), Alcohol Treatment Agencies or Substance Misuse Departments, often accept self-referrals in addition to referrals from GPs, and some even offer a drop-in service that will attend to anyone who walks in off the street between certain hours. Members of the public can also ring for information and advice.

Help with cutting down

In addition to treating those who have previously had physical addictions and need to be completely dry, local community alcohol services are normally willing to help drinkers with psychological addictions work towards controlled drinking, if giving up is considered either unnecessary or unrealistic at that point in time. They often have multi-disciplinary staff, including both healthcare workers and social workers, and can offer a wide range of support services, including home-based, inpatient or day-attendance medical detox programmes, counselling and group work. They are also usually keen to support those affected by the drinking of partners and family members, by teaching them appropriate strategies for dealing with the problem drinker.

WORKING OUT A COMPROMISE

There is no need to book an appointment at the NHS-funded Croydon Community Drug and Alcohol Centre or to be referred by your GP. Between 10am and 12 noon on Mondays, Wednesdays and Fridays, local residents with drink problems can simply turn up and be seen free of charge.

The nurse or alcohol worker who conducts an hour-long initial assessment will, however, ask those who attend for permission to contact their GP to obtain their medical records. It is extremely unusual for anyone not to agree to this.

'We try and work out a compromise between what they want and what we believe is the best course of action.'

"The first thing we want to know is the type of drink problem dependency they have developed and what they want to do about it," explains Consultant Psychiatrist Dr. David Ball. "We need to establish whether there are any complicating factors such as physical ailments and depression, what level of support they have at home and whether they have got into trouble with the law. We then try and work out a compromise between what they want and what we believe is the best course of action."

"Our basic approach is to get people off the drink first and then try to find the underlying reasons. They may or may not discover what has been causing their drinking, but even if they don't find out they will still be happier from not drinking and more able to cope."

"But if someone simply wants to cut down," he continues "we are willing to help them and hope that they will agree to give up for at least a period if they fail. People often have to fail at cutting down first in order to realise that they need to give up."

If a medical detox is required, this may be arranged in the form of a two-week inpatient stay at an NHS hospital or in the form of an eight-day home detox. The latter, which could involve either the problem drinker attending the centre every day or being visited daily at home by one of the centre's nurses, will only be possible if the individual concerned has a supportive partner, relative or other carer.

> 'People often have to fail at cutting down first in order to realise that they need to give up.'

"Coming off alcohol can be dangerous even when you have been administered drugs," explains Dr. Ball. "People can still have withdrawal fits or suffer from hallucinations, so it is important that there is always someone there who can phone for help."

"But don't forget that a detox is just a safe way of getting you off alcohol and the real hard work begins once it has finished. In one sense it's similar to dieting in that the longer you go on for the easier it gets, and the risk of relapse certainly seems to reduce after five years."

The centre can offer a whole range of supportive counselling methods, including four-week day attendance programmes to kick-start recovery, followed by weekly individual sessions for up to a year. It also works closely with social services, which funds residential rehabilitation.

(For contact details, see Appendix 3, page 248.)

Residential rehab on the State

Whilst it can be possible to obtain State funding for residential rehabilitation, which can last for anything up to 18 months and take place in a completely different part of the country, it has to be said that the chances of doing so are normally slim unless you are determined to be exceptionally pushy.

Much will depend on what types of non-residential treatment you have received already and how likely you are to be considered to remain completely dry afterwards. An absence of serious psychiatric problems and other health issues is also more likely to increase your chances.

Non-residential treatment

There is a much higher chance of being accepted on non-residential programmes in the area you live in, which can take the form of group therapy, harm reduction or one-to-one counselling. (See Case Study of Rebecca Sampson, Chapter 4, page 85.) Whilst general counselling, which may be limited to 8 to 16 sessions, will normally be free, you may be required to pay in the region of £25 to £30 an hour for more alcoholic specific counselling if you have no charities in your area that offer it.

In some areas, it may be possible to receive a free medical detox on the State at the Accident & Emergency unit of your local NHS hospital or at your GP's surgery – or administered by your GP in your home – whilst in others you are likely to be referred to a local community alcohol service.

Although it can take up to two months to receive a State-funded medical detox in some regions, where it is available more immediately, there is a lot to be said for taking advantage of it because paying privately can be extremely expensive. A private medical detox at home involving a live-in nurse is likely to cost between £400 and £1,000 a day. Bearing in mind that you will probably need to pay for seven to nine days worth of treatment, it could work out just as expensive as spending a month in a private rehab clinic.

Finding the State-funded facilities available

Details of the State-funded alcohol treatment facilities available, and of the other relevant voluntary services and self-help groups present in your area, can be obtained from numerous different sources.

In many cases, your GP will be aware of what is available and will be in a position to make a suitable recommendation. But if they are not, or if you don't want details of your drink problem available on your medical records, most of these services will be listed in local phone directories. Alternatively, the helplines detailed in Chapter 1 (See page 11), and even some of the specialist intermediaries detailed on page 112, are willing to direct you to appropriate local organisations free of charge. A further useful source of information is a directory of local drug and alcohol treatment services available on the Home Office's website (See Appendix 3, page 248).

CASE STUDY: RECOVERY COSTING NOTHING MORE THAN COMMITMENT

Jeff Broughton was so financially stretched by the time he made the decision to quit, that paying for any kind of treatment was out of the question. Nevertheless, since using the support available from local State-funded services and self-help groups, he has remained completely dry for over a year.

Jeff, who is 37 and works as a business consultant, decided it was time to face the music when suffering the worst hangover he had ever experienced during a drink problem that dated back 10 years. Too ill to return to work on the Monday, he booked an appointment with his GP, who put him in touch with his local Alcohol Advisory Service.

> 'Once the process of recovery gains momentum you start to medicate from within and you don't care that you have made mistakes.'

The Alcohol Advisory Service, which he describes as "extremely helpful", unfortunately had a waiting list of 10 weeks but was able to refer him to another group called Options, which ran a free out-of-work-hours relapse prevention group.

"This was an excellent group session that gave plenty of tips and advice," he enthuses, "but they were another overstretched service. Ideally, I would have liked to have benefited from their counselling facilities in combination with the relapse group, but the waiting list for counsellors was months rather than weeks. Consequently, I attended AA meetings as well, and found these very comforting during the early weeks."

"I personally found that all these groups offered some things that I liked and others I didn't, and the key is to pick the best tools for the job. But I would stress that I also made some important lifestyle changes, based on reading about drink issues and drawing on my own knowledge."

One of the most important of these changes was to cut out any caffeine from his diet, by drinking decaffeinated coffee, avoiding coca cola and only eating chocolate in extreme moderation.

> 'I personally found that all these groups offered some things that I liked and others I didn't, and the key is to pick the best tools for the job.'

"Your body needs a lengthy break to heal, and caffeine just makes you more sensitive, hyper and paranoid. Paranoia can be a major problem when drying out, because the body's 'flight or fight' system is thinking that there is a danger and makes up reasons why it should not believe sensory input from the eyes. This can result in you attaching additional meaning to the movements and actions of others."

"Also make sure you take regular vitamin supplements, as getting hammered all the time will have used up virtually all your vitamin B reserves, and start building fresh fruit and vegetables into your diet. Once the process of recovery gains momentum, you start to medicate from within and you don't care that you have made mistakes because you are so glad to feel well again."

Jeff also stresses the importance of goal setting and advises writing down all the roles you were expected to play as well as the ones you would like to play in the future. List against each role its long-term and short-term goals, making sure that the list of tasks under each short-term goal is specific, measurable, attainable, relevant and time-limited.

Selecting the right private care

The choice available to those seeking private treatment for drink problems is enormous, with costs ranging from between £350 and £10,000 a week. But the good news is that the task of selecting the most appropriate and best value private treatment has been made much easier during the last few years by the emergence of a number of specialist intermediaries. These organisations use their expert knowledge of the marketplace to source the best treatment deals and will receive a commission from the provider for doing so, but the treatment will not cost you more than if you approached the provider directly.

Contacting one of the intermediaries detailed below can therefore save a great deal of time and effort and significantly reduce the risk of making a poor choice. Some are able to negotiate keener rates on some deals than others, so it can be worth trying more than one.

Specialist Intermediaries

- DryOutNow.com
  Tel: 0845 2308060
  www.dryoutnow.com

- Re-cover
  Tel: 0845 6036530
  www.re-cover.org.uk

- ADMIT Services
  Tel: 0845 3020404
  www.admitservices.co.uk

(For more detailed information on all three organisations see Appendix 3, pages 223 to 227.)

All these intermediaries can arrange private medical detoxes, counselling and stays in residential rehab clinics and provide free initial advice on which, if any, of these facilities are necessary in your particular case.

For some people there will be a need to remove themselves from their own environment, especially if they have emotional problems or little in the way of family support. An inpatient stay may therefore well be the answer. A motivated and co-operative person who doesn't need a detox may, on the other hand, be better off receiving private treatment as a day patient, and will be spared having to readjust to new surroundings as a result.

"I would always prefer not to institutionalise someone because it means they don't have to subsequently readjust again to the outside world. It's your own recovery, not just the clinic's doing."

Prof. Griffith Edwards, Emeritus Professor of Addiction Behaviour at the National Addiction Centre, Institute of Psychiatry, King's College London

Stays in private clinics can last anywhere between one week and nine months, but most people stay for between four and twelve weeks. Therapy is aimed at helping you to understand why you drink and to develop alternatives to drinking, eventually leading to a fulfilled life without alcohol. You will have to face up to a variety of difficult issues and may experience intense mood swings.

But residential rehab is not the right option for those who simply want to cut down their drinking. The vast majority of the clinics concerned demand a commitment to being completely dry and, with few exceptions, use a 12 Step based approach. Even Plymouth-based Broadreach House, which uses motivational psychology instead of a 12 Step approach, is heavily abstinence orientated and thoroughly recommends attending AA as part of aftercare.

"Research shows that those who spend longer than a month in rehab do better than those who spend less than a month. It also shows that those who have some form of aftercare, such as counselling or attending AA, do better than those who don't."

Dr. Bruce Trathen, Consultant Addiction Psychiatrist at DryOutNow.com

CASE STUDY: 'HERO' TACKLED IN SOUTH AFRICA

45-year-old engineer Nigel Cockburn instantly found his feet at The Priory in Roehampton as the regime, which involved getting up early and working until lights-out, reminded him of his time at boarding school. He soon became group leader of the alcohol treatment patients and undertook recovery on his own terms, even altering the timetable to suit himself.

"I worked hard to come 'top of the class' and lead from the front in everything, including group sessions," he explains. "I received a basic grounding in the 12 Steps of AA, but, whilst I can grasp a concept rapidly, I have a tendency to quickly get bored and to move on to something else more exciting."

"By the end, I was even questioning my happy outlook and determination to be top dog in a treatment centre and, although I had accepted that I had a serious drink problem on the inside, my outward behaviour still conveyed a false confidence. I seemed grounded in my recovery, but I was aware that I would struggle to stay sober in real life and had learned that my triggers for drinking covered the whole gamut of emotions, from misery to elation."

> 'Although I had accepted that I had a serious drink problem on the inside, my outward behaviour still conveyed a false confidence.'

Realising that he still needed further help after his month at The Priory in July 2006, Nigel opted for three months of secondary care immediately afterwards at the Oasis treatment centre in Plettenberg Bay, South Africa. The package was arranged by specialist intermediary Re-cover, which had also organised the Priory stay.

At Oasis, his façade of playing the hero and leader was tackled head-on. He was not allowed to go first in physical activities or to be captain in outdoor challenges, wore clothes he previously believed were worn by slackers and didn't shave for two weeks.

"My role as a purveyor of sound advice to others was also challenged," he continues. "I realised that my drinking was a symptom of underlying causes and that I was prone to addiction to other substances and even to other people, as in expecting a girlfriend to solve my life problems for me. These were some of my comfort zones that needed to be swept away to show that I could live a happy life without all these defences in place."

> 'There were days when I wished I was elsewhere, but I didn't wish I was in a pub.'

"The treatment took me to an extreme where I felt unsafe mentally but I was saved by finding my higher power. Having rediscovered my spiritual side, the 12 Steps and treatment began to make sense to my heart. I don't search for my old comfort zones anymore but look for a balance in life and only lead when I have to, not when I need to."

"I put my total trust in the counsellors," he continues. "I didn't always agree with their viewpoint but I was willing to try out the new behaviour they advised and look at weaknesses I had never admitted to having. There were days when I wished I was elsewhere, but I didn't wish I was in a pub."

Selecting private care yourself

Those who prefer to select their own private treatment rather than go through an intermediary will find details of private clinics and other organisations in Appendix 3 (see pages 228 to 247). Additionally, suitable addiction counsellors and psychotherapists can be obtained from the British Association for Counselling and Psychotherapy (www.bacp.co.uk).

But before committing yourself to any rehab deal, make sure you pay attention to the small print, particularly with regard to what the financial repercussions are if you decide to drop out before completing the course.

> "If you are paying upfront, it would be wise to have it in writing that you will be refunded for the weeks not attended, should you choose not to finish the programme. At some clinics you can receive up to 10% savings when paying the full amount upfront, and most reputable clinics will refund the remaining weeks should you leave early."
>
> David Gilmour, Co-founder of specialist intermediary Re-cover

Looking beyond the conventional

The options available for curing drink problems also extend well beyond the conventional methods that are widely recommended by the medical profession, self-help organisations and specialist intermediaries.

If a technique has proved successful for one other person, there is no reason why it shouldn't also work for you, so it is important to keep an open mind about even the most unlikely sounding approaches.

'The only statistic we care about is you. Whatever percentages of others have succeeded or failed to control their drinking is of no relevance.'

We have already seen how Dr. Surinder Kaur (See Chapter 4, page 78) has developed an innovative new scientific method involving the use of video games, and how Edmund Tirbutt (See Chapter 3, page 61) cured himself of the underlying problems that had caused his drinking by undergoing a course of hypnotherapy five years after he had given up drinking. Hypnotherapy has also been known to help some people give up the drink in the first place.

A LAST TRANCE SALOON?

Norwich-based hypnotist Rick Maczka, has found ways of helping to interrupt and replace patterns of behaviour and thinking by using a combination of hypnosis, which takes people into a trance state where they can access experiences and knowledge held within their subconscious mind, and techniques that can help them gain a greater understanding and control of their thoughts, feelings, behaviours and communications.

"Typically, I ask clients to make a diary of their drinking, which can then highlight their motivation to stop," he explains, "or it can even produce a motivation to stop as it potentially raises an unconscious habit, and often one that involves denial, to conscious awareness."

'Once I have enhanced their determination and motivation, I can remove triggers for the person's drinking.'

"I have to recognise whether a client is only contemplating change, is determined to change, or doing it for someone else," he continues, "and I will spend a long time asking them questions and will set them various tasks, because I want them to be an active participant in their recovery."

"Once I have enhanced their determination and motivation, I can remove triggers for the person's drinking, and I can regress them to the time when they unconsciously decided to be that way and get rid of that decision, and then deal with the part of the personality that wants to drink and get it to work alongside the part of the personality that doesn't want to drink."

For **contact details for Rick Maczka and other hypnotherapists see Appendix 3, page 266.**

Other unconventional methods that could be worth trying include acupuncture, cognitive behavioural therapy (CBT), Buddhist meditation and colonic irrigation. Even the power of prayer should certainly not be dismissed (See Case of Study Hugh Graham, Chapter 3, page 67), nor should spiritual healing or faith healing.

BEATING SPIRITS WITH THE SPIRITUAL

Spiritual healer David Cunningham, who practices in both Durham and West London, describes himself as offering a "beautiful non-chemical way of dealing with drink problems", and even the most ardent sceptic could do worse than give this approach a try if all else has failed.

David, who has been practising for 16 years and is a member of the National Federation of Spiritual Healers, imparts healing energy by placing his right hand over his patients' heads. Patients can be referred by the NHS or social services' infrastructures from any area of the UK, or accessed privately at a cost of £50 per hour-long session (£90 in London).

'Drink problems result from self-rejection and from feeling guilty and unloved, and I direct energy towards the areas that can correct this imbalance.'

He says, "Whenever I have treated people with drink problems I have made positive changes, and around half of them have kicked the habit completely. There is no need for them to believe in any religion, but they do need to believe that healing can work. My understanding is that drink problems result from self-rejection and from feeling guilty and unloved, and I direct energy towards the areas that can correct this imbalance."

"I talk quite a lot to my patients as well, which is an important part of the healing process. If they attend once a week, recovery can take anything between a few weeks and five months. It all depends how willing they are to change by looking at the past and talking about it."

For contact details for Dave Cunningham and other spiritual healers see Appendix 3, page 268.

Key points

- What State-funded help you get will depend a lot on the area you live in

- It will also depend on how hard you try to make your voice heard

- If you push hard enough it can even be possible to enter private rehab funded by the State

- Specialist intermediaries can source the most appropriate private treatment at no extra cost

- If you select your own rehab clinic, check the terms with regards to dropping out early

- Be prepared to look beyond the more conventional methods of treatment

- If any method has worked for one other person it could also work for you

Part 2

Helping Others

Chapter 6:
Helping Adults

Most people who have experienced living with, or trying to help someone with, a serious drink problem will vouch for the fact that continual nagging and confiscating and hiding drink simply doesn't work. This is because, as in most other walks of life, people normally need to make decisions for themselves. They are far more likely to do something if they feel they have made up their own minds as opposed to feeling that they are obliged to do it to keep someone else happy.

Although simple caring support can be helpful early on, once it is clear that the person is taking no responsibility for their actions, the priority should be to try and help them to come to the realisation that they need to help themselves. Some of the techniques for doing this outlined later in this chapter require considerable subtlety and patience and set great store on avoiding confrontation.

Confronting loved ones

There are, however, cases where confrontational behaviour from friends and loved ones has clearly worked. On page 134 we see how long-suffering Sarah Hamilton finally got her husband to start attending AA by threatening to leave him, and on page 61 we see how some home truths from a close friend proved sufficient for Edmund Tirbutt to vow never to touch another drop. Next, we also see how Jason Hendry turned his life around after receiving a "give up or go" ultimatum from his sister.

CASE STUDY: SAVED BY HIS SISTER

Jason Hendry had already lived in a hostel for the homeless, drunk Tennents Super for breakfast and had been told by a liver specialist that he had to stop drinking if he wanted to live. But it was not until his sister threatened to kick him out of her house that he actually found the motivation to give up.

"Like many people who drink, I knew it was bad for me, and my doctor and family had told me to quit the drink, but I didn't really see the point," he explains. "But only when I realised that I might lose the love of my sister, who was the most important person in my life, did I have a real reason to beat the problem."

"I know that some people find it very difficult to stop and take it day by day but, in hindsight, I actually found it quite easy. Because I was still living at my sister's, I knew that I would be found out if I drank, so that took away any incentive whatsoever."

> 'It was not until his sister threatened to kick him out of her house that he actually had the motivation to beat the problem.'

Jason, who is now 37, had first started drinking heavily when he 'came out' at the age of 20, because the gay scene was very much built on socialising and meeting people in pubs. But the weight that he put on as a direct result soon started to affect his self-confidence, and it was not long before he was habitually drowning his sorrows at home.

The problem was then compounded by a rather ridiculous career move that saw him go from being an advertising manager to becoming a publican, and after being hospitalised as a result of his drinking on several occasions, he became unable to hold down a job.

"The number of black-outs and holes in my memory were getting worse, as was my behaviour and the situations I was allowing myself to get into," he recalls. "Mentally, I was at an all-time low and I phoned my sister to let her know that I was sorry and that I was going to commit suicide. She persuaded me to move in with her, and when she threatened to kick me out unless I quit the alcohol, I stopped right there and then."

"I lost a huge amount of weight, my skin got a lot better and I started to see the good things about myself rather than focusing on the bad things all the time. I also realised how goddamned unbearable most drinkers are. They constantly tell you the same story over and over again, forgetting what they have said, uncontrollably spitting and getting in too close."

> 'I lost a huge amount of weight, my skin got a lot better and I started to see the good things about myself rather than focusing on the bad things all the time.'

Jason initially remained completely dry for three years but, because he now does a job he enjoys in the textile industry and has sorted out the underlying issues that caused his unhappiness, he has subsequently managed to revert to drinking in moderation.

He feels the keys to the success of his new regime are that he tries to avoid drinking at home or on his own, keeps busy and exercises regularly by going running and visiting the gym.

Family intervention

There is even a method, known as 'family intervention', where family members join together to confront a problem drinker all at the same time with pre-prepared scripts. They deliver a message to the effect that they love the drinker very much but that they have simply had enough and that it is essential that the individual concerned seeks medical help.

But this method, like any kind of direct confrontation from loved ones, is obviously a high-risk strategy, and should only be used as a last resort in conjunction with expert advice. If it goes wrong it could increase the sense of denial of the problem drinker or even tip them over the edge.

> "The family intervention method can work but is best if professionally supported, and should only be used with caution as it can be damaging if it goes wrong."
>
> Dr. Bruce Trathen, Consultant Addiction Psychiatrist at DryOutNow.com

A stitch in time saves nine

The chances of helping someone you know are, however, greatly increased if you can spot the telltale signs and address the problem early on, well before a psychological addiction is accompanied by a physical one. Indeed, friends and relatives can often spot a problem before the drinker themselves. Whilst it is not unusual for people to drink heavily following a traumatic event such as a bereavement or redundancy, a failure to return to normal drinking patterns after a few months should be regarded as cause for concern.

> "Anyone who has been drinking well over the recommended government limits for longer than six months should trigger serious warning bells."
>
> Alison Rogers, Chief Executive of the British Liver Trust

Once it has got to the stage that you are continually embarrassed by someone's behaviour, or that you feel there is a "third party in the marriage" (e.g. your partner seems to have become more interested in spending time with alcohol than with you), it is definitely time for them to get help.

Other classic symptoms to watch out for are changes in mood and personality, a decline in appearance and personal standards and defensive behaviour whenever the subject of their drinking is mentioned. Additionally, problem drinkers often have a tendency to try and blame those nearest and dearest to them for their predicament in order to try to protect a fragile sense of self-esteem. It is essential that you don't allow them to convince you that it's your problem.

> "The act of blaming someone for a problem is really the same as saying they can't sort it out because it's not their fault."
>
> Dr. Bruce Trathen, Consultant Addiction Psychiatrist at DryOutNow.com

Tipping off the GP

Life would be a lot easier for friends and relatives of problem drinkers if they were simply allowed to force them to seek professional help by handing them over to the authorities in a similar way to that in which they might treat a loved one who they believed was mentally ill. But it is not possible to detain someone under the Mental Health Act in the UK on the grounds of alcohol abuse.

What is not commonly realised, however, is that if you share the same GP as a problem drinker it could be possible to bring the matter to the GP's attention in a roundabout way. The GP could then look for subtle opportunities to discuss the matter with the patient and possibly persuade them to undergo tests.

Even if you don't share a GP, there is still much to be said for raising the matter with your own GP, because they may be able to provide you with valuable advice on how to handle the situation – even though they will not be able to discuss the matter with the problem drinker.

Persuading them to seek help

In cases where there is no shared GP, experts stress that the objective should be to get the person who has a drink problem to seek professional help as opposed to trying to act as some form of amateur therapist yourself. Even if you have training in addiction therapy, the fact that you have an emotional involvement with the problem drinker is likely to prevent you from taking a sufficiently objective view of their predicament.

> "Often people stuck in these situations can't see the wood for the trees and have very strong feelings about a partner or friend, so help has to come from outside."
>
> Dr. Francis Keaney, Consultant Addiction Psychiatrist, National Addiction Centre, Institute of Psychiatry, King's College London

The Holy Grail is for the drinker to accept that they at least might have a problem. If they are able to reach this conclusion, then they may be prepared to discuss the matter with a suitably qualified professional. But you are most unlikely to achieve this result by lecturing or nagging.

The essential trick is to get the person to feel they have made their own decision to seek help. This can be done by developing the approaches described below, but it may take months of patience and practice.

The first step

The first step is to try to feed back to the problem drinker inconsistencies that they make, but this must be done in a way that doesn't trigger any feelings of resistance. The key is to never directly disagree with them or pretend to agree with them, and to avoid making statements of fact.

But, whilst you should avoid criticism, you should still praise positive behaviours, as this will help increase the individual's sense of their ability to change their life for the better. There is, however, clearly a danger of being perceived as manipulative or patronising, so the praise must be reasonably subtle.

> **"You must aim to roll along with them, not becoming resistant but at the same time not giving in to them either."**
>
> Dr. Bruce Trathen, Consultant Addiction Psychiatrist at DryOutNow.com

The process of feedback will hopefully result in them slowly becoming ready to admit they have a problem, but they are most unlikely to do this unless you are someone they feel they have a high degree of empathetic understanding with and are prepared to open up to. Because you are trying to help them, the chances are that you have such an understanding or at least have had it in the past. It could be that you have lost any empathy you once had because years of abuse have taken their toll but, if so, you should try hard to remind yourself of what the person used to be like and to understand that they shouldn't be blamed because their drink problem has reached a point at which it has progressed largely beyond their conscious control.

Avoid statements of fact

If possible, try to avoid asking questions that require a straightforward "yes or "no" answer, although these are still very much better than making statements of fact. The examples below of how to respond and how not to respond have been designed by a leading addiction expert at specialist intermediary DryOutNow.com.

Example of Bad Response, only likely to drive drinker deeper into denial:

Drinker: "I've got a stinking headache this morning."

Helper: "Well you shouldn't drink so much then."

Drinker: "What do you mean?"

Helper: "I mean that you need to stop drinking."

Example of Good Response:

Drinker: "I've got a stinking headache this morning."

Helper: "Is it a bad one?"

Drinker: "I think I'd better take the day off work."

Helper: "Will they mind?"

Drinker: "They said it could be a disciplinary next time, didn't they."

Helper: "Why's that?"

Drinker: "Too many days sick."

Helper: "Do you think you've taken too many days sick?"

Note that in the 'good response', the helper has demonstrated concern but has completely avoided talking about alcohol and has generally avoided saying anything that could be construed as a criticism. This could well result in the drinker wondering whether they have in fact taken too many days off. If the dialogue continues along similar lines, the drinker could therefore begin to consciously register that drinking could actually be a problem, although the chances are that they will insist on continuing to deny the fact verbally.

Don't change your behaviour

Needless to say, if you find yourself in physical danger you may have no option other than to phone the police or leave the premises. Otherwise, in order to motivate a drinker to contemplate the possibility that they might need help, you must behave in a way that leads them to take personal responsibility for their actions. The best way of achieving this is to aim to neither help them nor to hinder them and to continue to behave as normally as possible. For example, if you don't normally lock the door at night then don't lock it just because they come back drunk, because doing so is likely to create a sense of injustice. The idea is to get the person with a drink problem to conclude that there is no one to blame other than themselves for the consequences of their actions. Similarly, if they fall asleep on the sofa and are incontinent during the night, you shouldn't offer to help them clean themselves or to wash the sofa, because they should be allowed to experience the consequences of this behaviour without others interfering.

> 'Continual nagging and confiscating and hiding drink simply doesn't work.'

If you find drink hidden in the house or even sitting staring everyone in the face in the kitchen, then just leave it where it is because it is the responsibility of the individual you are trying to help to decide whether or not to drink. If, on the other hand, they ask you to buy alcoholic drinks for them you should refuse, because they need to be taking responsibility for all aspects of their drinking, including buying their drink.

If you have to leave

Even if you reach the point at which you decide that you simply cannot carry on living with a problem drinker any more, you may still feel that you want to help them. If so, you should make a point of explaining that you are only leaving as a direct consequence of their drinking and that, apart from this, you have no problems with them as a person. You should make it clear that only they can help themselves and that you will still be available to support them if they decide to seek help. But you should make it equally clear that your potential support is dependent on them making the first move.

Giving some options

If, and only if, you reach that crucial stage when the drinker is willing to admit that they could possibly have a problem with alcohol, will you be in a position to start offering them some potential solutions. But, if you attempt to do so before they have indicated that they are ready to receive advice, you could simply push them further into denial.

> 'The Holy Grail is for the drinker to accept that they at least might have a problem.'

You must not under any circumstances try to rush or force the situation, but if they do reach the point of admitting the possibility of a problem, you must make sure that you are in a position to capitalise on the situation.

If, for example, the drinker asks whether you think they are drinking too much, they have provided you with a golden opportunity to steer the conversation around. You would now be at a point where you could volunteer some advice if you follow the non-confrontational approach below devised by the same DryOutNow.com expert.

Non-Confrontational Approach

Drinker: "Why, do you think I'm drinking too much?"

Helper: "Well, looking from the outside, it does seem to be the cause of a few problems you're having. I mean I might be wrong. What do you think?"

Drinker: "I'm not sure."

Helper: "I can say that you haven't looked very well to me for quite some time now. Do you feel ill?"

Drinker: "I'm feeling worn out the whole time."

Helper: "Is there anything you'd like me to do?"

Drinker: "What can you do – what is there to do?"

Helper: "Well maybe we should try to find out if drinking has got anything to do with this or not – maybe it has, maybe it hasn't."

Drinker: "And how are we going to do that?"

Helper: "If I find out some information, I could leave it with you to have a look at."

Drinker: "And how's that going to help?"

Helper: "I don't know; could it do any harm?"

Drinker: "I suppose not."

Having got so far, try leaving some independently written material the next day for the problem drinker to read. But you must then be prepared to wait for them to bring the subject up again. If they do so, you can respond by suggesting a few options, like contacting their GP, phoning the helplines detailed in Chapter 1 (page 11), or contacting the specialist intermediaries detailed in Chapter 5 (page 112).

> 'As in most other walks of life, people normally need to make decisions for themselves.'

But you must leave the problem drinker to make their own decision with regard to which one of these options they pursue. If it turns out that they are not ready to follow up on any of them, then you mustn't try to force the issue. You can at least take heart from the fact that the drinker has started to contemplate that there may be a problem and that this should count positive if the subject arises again in the future.

CASE STUDY: HANDING BACK RESPONSIBILITY

"I had threatened several times to leave him if he didn't phone AA, but he realised I wasn't being serious," explains 44-year-old Sarah Hamilton. "But then one day I really meant it and told him I had completely given up and it was now finally over."

"I knew I had run out of energy and I felt that my efforts to stop him drinking were preventing him from taking responsibility for his own problems. I had become his conscience and he relied on that."

On that occasion five years ago, Sarah, who works as an administrator and lives in north London, had not even bothered to mention AA. But the move certainly had the desired effect on her husband David. The 40-year-old advertising executive has since been attending AA meetings regularly and, despite the odd relapse, has been sober.

'I felt that my efforts to stop him drinking were preventing him from taking responsibility for his own problems.'

Sarah advises never arguing with a problem drinker when they are drunk because it just makes things worse, as does trying to stop them drinking at any point.

She says "If an argument starts you should leave the room, and you shouldn't hide bottles, pour drink down the sink or try and stop them when they say they are going out for a drink. It can be tempting to do all of these things but none of them work. I went teetotal myself for four years, but even that didn't help."

"In fact, if anything, it even seemed to wind him up because he knew I didn't have his illness and therefore felt a bit patronised. Now I never drink in front of him, but I don't mind him knowing I'm going for a drink and even seeing me coming back a bit tipsy, although I may avoid doing so if I feel he is approaching a relapse."

"It's also important to remember that you didn't cause the problem, you can't cure it and you can't control it," she continues. "It's not your fault, although those with drink problems often try and blame their partners."

'You shouldn't hide bottles, pour drink down the sink or try and stop them when they say they are going out for a drink.'

Sarah has found it much easier to switch off from her domestic problems since joining Al-Anon, which has enabled her "to find peace and serenity". She says she will attend it for the rest of her life, even if David never drinks again or dies before her, because she would still want to pass on her advice to others.

"Attending the first meeting took all my courage," she explains, "but speaking to people who have had similar experiences gives you hope. A lot of them have helped their alcoholic partners, friends or relations by avoiding unnecessary arguments and handing back responsibility to them."

"Al-Anon has completely transformed me as a person and I have a lot more confidence now. Living with someone with a serious drink problem had made me feel so irritable and frustrated that I became part of the problem."

Further information on how Al-Anon and other self-help groups can help the friends and relatives of those with drink problems, and how Alateen and other organisations can help the children of those with drink problems, can be found in Chapter 8.

Key points

- Beware of anyone drinking well over the government guidelines for more than six months

- Nagging and confiscating or hiding drink doesn't work

- The priority is to get the person with the drink problem to realise they need to seek help

- Confrontation can work in some circumstances but involves serious risks

- If you share the same GP you can bring the matter to the GP's attention

- The Holy Grail is for the drinker to accept that they might have a problem

- If you have to stop living with a problem drinker, make it clear it is because of the drink and not because of them as a person

Chapter 7:
Helping The Young

The fact that it is illegal for someone aged under 18 to buy alcohol does little to prevent it from being regularly consumed by those many years younger. 15 and 16 year-olds, particularly physically mature girls, can easily manage to get themselves served in pubs and clubs, and even 11 and 12 year-olds seem to have no difficulty in getting friends to buy alcohol for them. Indeed, we have an absurd situation in which the drinks industry is effectively setting out to encourage underage drinking through the provision of alcopops.

> **"I'm particularly concerned about alcopops, for which I feel there is no justification. They have been specifically manufactured to make alcohol taste pleasant to children, and one of the very few safeguards we have is that alcohol is an acquired taste and most children think the flavour is disgusting."**
>
> Esther Rantzen, Founder of ChildLine

Cirrhosis of the liver, having previously been regarded as a middle-aged person's disease that took 10 to 30 years to develop, is consequently now being found in some problem drinkers who are still in their late teens. Furthermore, the gender gap has disappeared and problem drinkers are just as likely to be girls these days.

Unfortunately, adolescents, whose brains are going through a period of dynamic change, need to drink much less than adults to suffer the same negative effects. Teenage drinking can therefore seriously damage the growing process and impair learning and memory. It can also greatly increase the chances of drink problems developing in adulthood.

> "We know that youngsters who drink under the age of 14 are more likely to develop drink problems later in life."
>
> Alison Rogers, Chief Executive of the British Liver Trust

Alcohol is one of the most common causes of death of people aged under 30, as it is linked to many suicides and accidents. Problem drinking also greatly increases the chances of teenagers getting involved with crime. Whilst it doesn't lead to anything like the level of theft that can result from the need to fund usage of drugs like heroin and crack cocaine, it can often result in assault, drunken and disorderly behaviour and drink-driving offences.

It also leads to an increased risk of pregnancy by resulting in reduced use of contraception. According to ChildLine, which provides a confidential telephone counselling service for children with problems of every sort, alcohol is frequently cited by callers as a factor associated with unprotected sex leading to pregnancy. Young people who phone the service rarely blame other drugs in relation to unwanted pregnancy. Parents, who tend to have a disproportionate fear of illegal drugs, must therefore realise that children put themselves at real risk of harm via alcohol in many ways.

> "Parents should take alcohol seriously. It's very common for them to sit at home, biting their fingernails to the quick worrying about children taking drugs and to breathe a huge sigh of relief when a child arrives home helplessly drunk instead."
>
> Prof. Ian Gilmore, President of the Royal College of Physicians

Research shows that young people don't just drink in order to imitate adult behaviour. Some do so to cope with stress or simply to put them in a good mood, whilst others see drink more as a fashion statement and perceive it as having a valuable role to play in forming relationships with others. It can, for example, help sexual relationships by removing inhibitions and can help with bonding and developing trust with friends.

Experts also stress that parents should realise that it is normal for most teenagers to go through an experimental phase and that this is certainly likely to involve them getting drunk once in a while.

> "It's unrealistic to expect most teenagers not to get drunk occasionally. Trying to stop them would be like Canute trying to hold back the waves."
>
> Alison Rogers, Chief Executive of the British Liver Trust

Nevertheless, parents should certainly start getting worried if they find a child is drinking secretly or overtly and continuously – e.g. if they are demonstratively proud of the fact that they are getting completely wrecked at least once a week.

If they are truanting from school, they are likely to be in a high-risk group and may also be exposed to other problems like cannabis.

It is also important to note that teenagers who smoke are more likely to drink heavily than those who don't, and it can be easier to spot the signs of addictive smoking than of addictive drinking.

Setting the right example

Because a lot of behaviour is learned in the home, parents who wish to avoid finding that their children have drink problems should first take a long hard look at their own drinking habits. There is no doubt that heavy drinking parents have a tendency to produce children who become heavy drinkers.

"There is strong evidence to show parents' own attitudes towards alcohol and their supervision of its use with the family can have a significant impact on their children's attitude towards alcohol."

Richard Kramer, Director of Policy at Turning Point

Parental drinking habits can even have a significant future impact on children before they are born. Some research, for example, suggests that pregnant mothers who enjoy three or more alcoholic drinks during the same session, more than double the chances of their children developing a drinking disorder during their teens – making the new government guidelines that pregnant women should avoid alcohol altogether seem eminently logical.

CASE STUDY: IT ALL STARTED IN CHILDHOOD

Becky Massow did not attend her first AA meeting until the day after her 30th birthday, but she now realises that the first seeds of the drink problem she has defeated were sown before she had even started primary school.

"I first tasted beer when I was around six years of age" she explains. "I used to go to the local pub opposite our family home with my dad and join in what I believed was fun. Everyone looked happy, my dad was well liked and, because I was his daughter, I was popular too. I remember feeling really proud of my dad as everyone seemed to like him, and I loved being with him."

"He would let me take the froth off his beer and I would sneak sips when he went to the bar for another round. I enjoyed the taste but, more importantly, I enjoyed the feelings of popularity, happiness and love that I got from being with my dad. I believe my behaviour started to change the day I took those first sips."

> 'She now realises that the first seeds of the drink problem she has defeated were sown before she had even started primary school.'

By the time Becky had started university she had come to hate the world and everything in it, and had even contemplated suicide. To escape her feelings of anger and resentment she began drinking heavily, mainly on her own but with the notable exception of when she was with her father – who had since left her mother.

"I would binge drink when I was with my dad" she recalls. "I felt hurt because I wanted him to love me as he did when I was six, but I now know that what I wanted was impossible for someone with the same illness. I would cling to him and block anyone who I felt threatened that relationship."

"I would be untrusting of any female who came into contact with him and my behaviour ensured that no-one else was about when I was. I was selfish, needy and demanded attention, just like the six-year-old that I once was."

> 'I believe my behaviour started to change the day I took those first sips.'

At the age of 30, after Becky had achieved four months of sobriety through attending AA meetings, she underwent a free treatment programme with Stockport-based charity the Alcohol & Drug Abstinence Service (ADAS). This addressed the irrational feelings of anger she was experiencing, despite having quit the drink.

ADAS told her that the treatment would be the hardest thing she would ever do but also the best, and, in retrospect, she believes that to be true. When Becky first quit the drink she had questioned whether she could stay sober during occasions such as birthdays, funerals and Christmas, but she soon learned that this was possible. Indeed, her mother actually died during the ADAS treatment period, but the experience didn't tempt her to drink.

"I knew that I was in the right place and that I would be okay," she explains. "I knew a drink wouldn't bring my mum back and that I did not want that life back, and I still don't want that life back today."

The importance of education

One of the problems with telling a teenager not to do something is that you can bet your bottom dollar that it will result in them ending up doing it even more. But there is a difference between imparting educational messages and nagging.

> "It's very difficult for parents to scrutinise children's habits all the time. The important thing is for children to be educated in the dangers of alcohol."
>
> Esther Rantzen, Founder of ChildLine

Research studies have shown that adolescents who believe that drinking alcohol has many positive and few negative consequences are likely to start drinking earlier and more frequently than those who develop more negative expectancies. The emphasis should therefore be on providing useful information on the dangers of alcohol from an early age and on setting a suitable example.

But make sure that the negatives are things that are relevant to their lives now, because telling a teenager that they might be storing up problems for when they are 40 is likely to be a waste of time – although their outlook can change significantly in this respect once they reach their 20s (See Case Study of Robert Power, pages 148 to 149).

> "Don't try and frighten an adolescent that they will get damage to their liver or heart when they are much older. Concentrate more on the immediate and more personal effects of alcohol, such as accidents, the horrors of drink-driving, sexual health risks and the effects of alcohol on weight and skin."
>
> Dr. Eilish Gilvarry, Consultant in Addiction Psychiatry (expert on adolescents)

Effective communication

By all means have a glass of wine with your children over a meal. Indeed, some research suggests that the children of parents who do so are less likely to develop drink problems when they grow older, because incorporating alcohol use into family life in a safe and supervised way is normally a safer approach than mystifying it. But alcohol should never be something that you consume all evening, every evening, in front of children.

There is some evidence which suggests that it can pay to be open and honest when communicating about alcohol to children and to make references to personal experience. There is also a lot to be said for keeping in touch with other parents and sharing information about alcohol misuse.

Most experts stress that the best advice that parents can take on board is to be aware of the importance of getting to know their children and being prepared to talk to them about what is driving them to drink, what they are drinking and how they are managing to finance the habit.

"Think about who the young person is in relation to their life and their desire to express their individuality, and understanding of the drink will fall into place. What laughter and fears do they have and how do they respect themselves in general? We don't talk to our young people enough about these things. We are afraid of being pompous and intrusive but such a conversation can be mutually beneficial. Try and talk to them, and if you don't succeed the first time keep at it."

Prof. Griffith Edwards, Emeritus Professor of Addiction Behaviour at the National Addiction Centre, Institute of Psychiatry, King's College London

Facing up to responsibilities

There are, however, also some straightforward practical safeguards that parents should be implementing to reduce the exposure of children, particularly those in their early teens, to alcohol. When children say they are staying overnight with friends, parents should actually phone the friend's parents to confirm that this will be the case, and check whether adults are going to be present and whether drink is going to be allowed. It is also better to allow 15 or 16-year-olds one drink with the family before they go out, than to half-knowingly allow them to drink on their own in their rooms whilst getting ready.

"Parents have responsibilities. Bringing up children to walk and talk is one thing, but getting through adolescence is also part of it. They need to support children to have both wings and roots. Adolescents want to be independent, though they need parents' support and guidance."

Dr. Eilish Gilvarry, Consultant in Addiction Psychiatry (expert on adolescents)

Taking action

Be watchful and non-judgmental, studying carefully the drinking patterns that children are setting, and, if you feel there is a problem, don't panic because confrontation is only likely to make things worse. The emphasis should be on tackling the issue sensitively but head-on. But this does not mean broaching the subject when the youngster is under the influence of alcohol. Leave it until the next day. If they come home drunk, put them to bed and make sure they are safe, although if they are grossly intoxicated you may have to take them to the Accident and Emergency unit at your local hospital.

If there are clearly problems with "getting through", referring children to ChildLine (Tel: 0800 11 11) can give them the chance to talk in the strictest confidence about their drink problem to qualified counsellors. Alternatively, 180 different young people's substance misuse services are listed on a special directory, aimed at helping people under the age of 18, on the National Treatment Agency's (NTA) website (See Appendix 3, page 247).

A further useful source of support is Youngaddaction, an offshoot of the Addaction charity (See Appendix 3, page 238).

Often self-correcting

There can clearly come a point when tough love has to be used but, fortunately, age is often an effective cure. Many young people tone down their drinking as soon as they leave university and, as we see in the case study below, even those that don't, can find that their perspective on life starts to change quite significantly during their 20s.

CASE STUDY: TRAVELLING ENDS TEENAGE PROBLEM

By the time Robert Power had reached the ripe old age of 19, he was downing a litre of whisky a day, mostly on his own. The slippery slope had started with wine and beer two years earlier when his father was diagnosed with multiple sclerosis and, to make matters worse, a girl Robert would like to have gone out with upset him by sleeping with his mate.

The habit helped create financial problems, which resulted in Robert, now a 27-year-old mature student at London University, actually becoming bankrupt. It could also well have cost him his life by now if he had not managed to address the problem eight years ago.

The decision to cut down was taken before leaving to go travelling in Australia with a friend, as he was concerned about finding himself in a position in which he could have a huge problem if he couldn't find a bar. He didn't require medical help or the assistance of any self-help group.

> 'When I was 18 I didn't care if I died when I was 30, but now I certainly do.'

The fact that Robert suffered no withdrawal symptoms the morning after not drinking for the first night in two and a half years, meant that he had not yet developed a physical addiction. But someone else drinking so heavily could easily have done so, and could therefore have caused themselves serious harm by stopping without a medical detox.

By the time he had returned from six months of travelling in Australia, during which time he drank very little, he had shed seven stone in weight. The psychological dependence on alcohol had also been broken, and his life was well and truly back on track.

Although he still drinks heavily at weekends and moderately on Thursday evenings, he only does so in the company of other people and doesn't touch a drop between Sunday and Wednesday.

"The cracking point was the travelling, as it was so inspirational knowing that there is more to life than coming home and having a glass of something before taking my coat off and experiencing that warm feeling again," he explains. "It also has a lot to do with growing up, because when I was 18 I didn't care if I died when I was 30, but now I certainly do."

"Even if I had all the money in the world, I would never go back to drinking during the week because I refuse to be addicted. I would just drink better wine at weekends."

'It was so inspirational knowing that there is more to life than coming home and having a glass of something before taking my coat off and experiencing that warm feeling again.'

"But I could never have envisaged giving up completely," he continues, "and I find people who say that abstinence is the only way extremely irritating. Someone who is obsessive might need to quit completely but I'm an easy-going person, and ultimately it's down to the personality of the individual."

Although Robert is still drinking at weekends at levels that could be causing him physical harm, experts emphasise that he has still achieved a noteworthy "result", and that the four days a week on which he doesn't drink are giving his liver a chance to repair the damage he is causing himself.

Key points

- Problem drinkers are now just as likely to be girls as boys

- Teenage drinking can damage the growing process and impair learning and memory

- It can also greatly increase the chances of drink problems developing in adulthood

- It is unrealistic to expect most teenagers not to get drunk once in a while

- Parental drinking habits can have a huge impact on children

- Be prepared to talk to your children about why they are drinking

- The emphasis should be on tackling the subject sensitively but head-on

Chapter 8:
If Only...

Unfortunately, those with drink problems do not only harm themselves. Indeed, in some cases they arguably cause even more hurt to partners, friends and family members who are not continually anaesthetising their own pain by consuming alcohol. Furthermore, those who try to help problem drinkers on a long-term basis can become "co-dependent", meaning that they become as compulsive and unwell as the person that they have been trying to help.

> "You don't have to be a problem drinker to suffer from problem drinking. Families, both individually and collectively, can become almost as consumed by an alcohol problem as the person doing the drinking. In the process, they can suffer immense stress and lose sight of their own needs. However, with the right support they can recover themselves."
>
> Nick Barton, Joint Chief Executive of Action on Addiction

The hurt and impact caused to those who know and love the problem drinker can come from two main sources. On the one hand, there are the direct results of the drinker's actions, such as their abusive behaviour, their constant stream of excuses for their drinking and denials about it, their ability to be a continuous source of embarrassment, their attempts to shift the blame for their problems onto others and their need for emotional and financial support.

On the other hand, there is the guilt that can result from feeling that you could have done more to help them combat their addiction earlier on, and the ongoing anxiety resulting from feeling unable to improve their current state.

As we can see from the moving case study of 55-year-old Jennie Eccleston, even a problem in the most casual of acquaintances can have a profound effect on someone's life, and leave them with a lingering feeling that they should have acted differently.

CASE STUDY: IF ONLY I'D MADE THAT CALL...

One day in the late 1970s, Jennie Ecclestone returned to her office to find the atmosphere curiously strained. The general manager had just sacked his new personal assistant, who had arrived for work that morning an hour late, clothes askew, make-up smudged and very drunk. She was still lying in a heap on the floor.

Jennie, a 55-year-old marketing director in the fashion industry, recalls "She whimpered and sobbed as I made a feeble attempt at calming her down and sobering her up with a coffee. As the mascara poured down her face, she begged me to get her job back for her because her money had run out and it was all she had left. But the general manager had already rung the agency for a replacement, so she was history. I had never had to deal with a situation like this before."

"I was given her address and told to drive her home. The small garden in front of the property was overgrown and neglected and the house behind the front door was a complete mess. I made her more coffee and, as I couldn't leave her in this condition, I stayed for a while. Gradually she told me about herself."

'This time she had decided she was finally going to make a new start and stop drinking.'

"Drink had led to divorce and she had been refused access to her daughters by the court," Jennie continues. "One by one her family and friends had given up on her, and she freely admitted that she had abused their love and friendship, but this time she had decided she was finally going to make a new start and stop drinking."

As she was leaving, Jennie suggested that she gave her a call at the office, once she had sorted herself out and found a new job. She never did. But Jennie didn't ring her either, and had largely forgotten about her, when two years later she received a telephone call from the police, who had been called to a "domestic". The former PA had given the police Jennie's name as the only person she knew.

'I still wonder whether things might not have worked out differently if I had bothered to call her all those years ago.'

"The housing estate was grim and the staircase to the flat stank of urine and was strewn with hideous litter. A policewoman greeted me as I approached the front door and questioned me. I told her that apart from the few hours I had been with my former colleague on the day she was sacked, I had spent little more than half an hour in her company in the office."

"I scarcely recognised my self-appointed friend who, barely conscious, refused to talk to me. On the way out, the young policewoman observed how strange it was that, in spite of all the filth, the woman had somehow managed to keep my business card absolutely pristine. She wondered why she had kept it and why she hadn't called me before. I still wonder whether things might not have worked out differently if I had bothered to call her all those years ago."

If only I'd...

With partners, close friends and members of immediate family, such feelings of guilt are inevitably magnified many times over. The natural reaction is to always try to search for a reason to explain the individual's drinking, and more often than not this will involve some element of self-blame.

If only we hadn't sent him to that school or university...if only I told him what I really thought when he said he was thinking of marrying that bitch...the list is endless.

In some cases, by using the methods outlined in Chapter 6, it may have been possible to have persuaded your loved one to seek professional help. But the overriding thing to bear in mind is that nagging or confiscating or hiding drink simply doesn't work. Whether you decide to put up with the situation, stand up to it with tough love or to withdraw and become more independent from the person suffering, you are still likely to have some contact with them. The essential trick is to get the person to feel they have made their own decision to seek help.

> 'The Holy Grail is for the drinker to accept that they at least might have a problem. If they are able to reach this conclusion, then they may be prepared to discuss the matter with a suitably qualified professional.'

We have also seen that there certainly have been cases where more confrontational approaches from friends and loved ones have worked, but this is a much higher risk strategy because there is always the fear that the problem drinker could feel resentment or humiliation, and end up drinking even more than they were doing in the first place. In a worst case scenario, they could even end up taking their own life, leaving those who delivered the harsh words with a permanently troubled conscience.

Fear of the consequences of intervention undoubtedly represents the single biggest reason for friends and loved ones failing to take a stance that, with the benefit of hindsight, they often wish they had taken. But this fear certainly deserves to be taken seriously, and each case must be considered on its own merits.

The potential guilt that can result from not acting appropriately must be carefully weighed up against the potential guilt that could result from taking that very action.

No great loss

Another common fear that often prevents people from trying to help problem drinkers is that they are worried that they will lose the individual's friendship if their efforts are met with hostility. This fear is far less logical because, although true friends are certainly hard to replace, you have effectively already lost any friend that has a serious physical addiction. They are likely to be a source of constant concern, hurt and embarrassment to you, and will frequently be telling you lies. From a purely selfish viewpoint you are therefore actually likely to be better off without them, even though your love and concern is likely to fuel a desire to see them cured and well.

Even if the drinker currently just has a psychological addiction and is still able to make a positive contribution to your life, you will effectively lose them as a friend if you allow the situation to deteriorate. There is, therefore, clearly a case for not being too concerned about the fact that a problem drinker may wish to see less of you if you insist on taking a firm stand. Why should you feel guilty as long as you pledge to support any moves they make to help themselves? You are arguably creating a win-win situation, increasing their chances of recovery and improving your own quality of life.

> 'You should make it clear that only they can help themselves and that you will still be available to support them if they decide to seek help. But you should make it equally clear that your potential support is dependent on them making the first move.'

Setting the right example

If you continue to see a problem drinker regularly and feel unable to coax them into seeking professional help, setting the right example may at least help you to live with yourself more easily, even if it ultimately does little to help them.

One common regret expressed by many people who have lost loved ones through drink is that they wished that they had never drunk in front of them. Whilst your actions might not change those of the drinker, you can at least help to demonstrate that it is possible to lead a full and active life without the prop of alcohol.

"But if only I had shown some leadership during the earlier stages when their addiction was primarily psychological then maybe, just maybe, they would have realised that I was being serious about their need to change."

Lucy Hogarth (See Case Study, page 165)

But there is clearly a right way and a wrong way of taking this approach. If your own unwillingness to drink in front of them is continually accompanied by lectures about the need for the problem drinker to correct their own behaviour, it is only likely to backfire.

Indeed, even if you decide to give up drinking alcohol completely – regardless of whether the problem drinker is present or not – this can have a negative effect on the drinker if it is made clear that it has been done largely for their benefit. In Chapter 6, for example, we saw how 44-year-old Sarah Hamilton's decision to go teetotal for four years seemed to be of little help to her husband.

"In fact, if anything, it even seemed to wind him up because he knew I didn't have his illness and therefore felt a bit patronised."

Sarah Hamilton (See Case Study, Chapter 6, page 134)

Nevertheless, explaining to a problem drinker that you are not drinking simply because you have decided that you don't enjoy it or that the habit wasn't doing you any good, can at least help you feel much better about yourself. You will doubtless be accused of being a "bore", but it will not take long to work out which party is actually the boring one!

CASE STUDY: IF ONLY I HADN'T JOINED IN...

43-year-old Peter Whetton has always lived with the nagging feeling that he could have done something to prevent the tragic demise of his university chum Jim, who died of cirrhosis of the liver in 2005.

Whilst Peter, who is now a chartered accountant, is aware that attempting to confront friends with drink problems can often be a futile activity, he has certainly read of cases where it has actually worked and, at the very least, he wishes that he had not proved such a willing drinking companion for Jim at university and beyond.

But his friend was funny, entertaining and always living the life of an artist. He was a poet come novelist in the drunken Irish literary mould. Those who knew him realised that his behaviour was wrong in a way, but they justified it with the knowledge that everyone got drunk and that Jim just did it more than everyone else.

'When anyone whips out a booze story, with Jim in your memory bank you can trump it just like that. You are his agent, thriving on his boozing.'

"The more you and everyone else keep the dream alive, the longer it goes on, through the early years of social drinking and into the hardwiring of the brain into real addiction," Peter explains. "But if everyone had said 'no' and there had been no-one for Jim to report back to from the outer limits, he might have seen his drinking for what it really was."

"You think you are doing him a favour by not confronting him, but you aren't. His belief system seems more interesting than yours, and in some ways it probably is, but on the glamorisation of drinking you are both wrong. You know it deep down inside and perhaps he does too. Something inside you realises that getting drunk all day every day just isn't going to work. You will be proved right 10 years down the line and Jim will agree with you, but by then it will be too late."

'The more you and everyone else keep the dream alive, the longer it goes on, through the early years of social drinking and into the hardwiring of the brain into real addiction.'

"So, for the time being you keep on backing his world view, sustaining the buzz of his out-there life experience, but for what?" he continues. "So you can tell your friends that you know a real hard-core boozer. When anyone whips out a booze story, with Jim in your memory bank you can trump it just like that. You are his agent, thriving on his boozing, and you don't even have to buy the drinks."

"He is also a good friend who feels for you and wants to protect you and who always has good advice. He seems very clever and the candle of his mind burns so brightly you feel unsure about telling him he is wrong. If you believe in the pleasure principle you can feel the stupid one sitting there sober, because even if he is dead by 40 he will have had more big nights than you, and isn't that what life's all about?"

Accepting defeat

Whilst it is clearly important to do everything you feel you can do to help a loved one with a drink problem, there may well come a point when you feel that you simply cannot do any more.

If we are talking about a serious physical addiction, it can certainly be helpful at this stage to take the view that the drinker is suffering from a disease that both you and them are powerless to combat. This can help you to detach yourself from the situation and to get on with focusing on your own life without continuing to be plagued by guilt.

> "Sometimes you may have to accept the fact that there is nothing you can do or could have done. You are not omnipotent."
>
> Dr. Francis Keaney, Consultant Addiction Psychiatrist, National Addiction Centre, Institute of Psychiatry, King's College London

From now on, the primary focus should be on helping yourself and, because there is currently little in the way of State help available for families and friends of problem drinkers, joining Al-Anon or another appropriate self-help group could prove the most effective solution.

Al-Anon

Al-Anon is a national and international network of self-help groups that helps the families and friends of problem drinkers put the focus back on themselves in a healthy loving way by providing understanding, strength and hope. There is no charge for attending meetings (although most groups make a collection to cover expenses), and only first names are used by attendees in order to help protect anonymity.

Al-Anon believes alcoholism is a family illness and that shared experiences and changed attitudes can enable the situation to be improved for everyone concerned, and may even encourage the drinker to recognise the problem and seek help if they haven't already done so. Regardless of whether or not the problem drinker has found sobriety, Al-Anon may be able to help you if you answer "yes" to some of the questions below.

CAN AL-ANON HELP?

- Am I worried?
- Am I losing sleep?
- Do I feel sorry for myself, inadequate or guilty?
- Am I ashamed of my situation?
- Do I ever feel embarrassed by the drinker's behaviour?
- Do I make excuses for the drinker and take on their responsibilities?
- Am I tired, nervous, depressed?
- Am I short-tempered and frustrated at times?
- Do I ever feel desperate and alone?

The basic philosophy is that only those who have lived with someone with a serious drink problem and have experienced the mental anguish that goes with it, can understand the problem of the drinker's family and friends, and that once you realise you are powerless over alcohol you are freed from a staggering burden.

Meetings, which normally last around one and a half hours, are usually opened with a moment of silence and closed with a prayer, and are led by a chairman who calls on members to tell others how Al-Anon helps them. But no one present is actually compelled to speak. If they prefer, they can just listen.

> "Al-Anon has completely transformed me as a person and I have a lot more confidence now. Living with someone with a serious drink problem had made me feel so irritable and frustrated that I became part of the problem."
>
> Sarah Hamilton (See Case Study, Chapter 6, page 134)

As with AA (See Chapter 3, pages 53 to 55), the programme is spiritual but not religious, and it involves detailed discussion of 12 Steps that have been adapted from AA.

Contact details

Details of Al-Anon meetings in your area can be obtained from the contact details given in Appendix 3 (page 250) or, if there is no Al-Anon group near you, you can start your own. Any two or three relatives or friends of problem drinkers can do this, provided that as a group they have no other affiliation outside of Al-Anon.

Alternatively, Co-dependents Anonymous (CoDA) provides a further option (See Appendix 3, page 256), and details of local support groups can also be obtained from Adfam (See Appendix 3, page 244).

Alateen

Similar support for the children of those with drink problems can be found through Alateen, which is part of Al-Anon. Members, who can be aged between 12 and 17, recognise that they are no longer alone and learn about alcoholism as a family illness (See Appendix 3, page 250). Useful information and support can also be obtained through the National Association for Children of Alcoholics (NACOA) – see Appendix 3, page 245.

> "I'm very pro Alateen. It's important that children in these situations recognise that they are not entirely alone."
>
> Esther Rantzen, Founder of ChildLine

CASE STUDY: IF ONLY I'D SET THE RIGHT EXAMPLE...

"If you're sick and tired of feeling sick and tired it's as good an indicator as any that you may have a drink problem," explains legal PA Lucy Hogarth, "and I've known several people who have managed to kick the habit completely once the realisation dawned on them."

But Lucy, who is 41 and lives in Birmingham, has also experienced watching two loved ones drink themselves to death in what she can only describe as "slow motion horror movies lasting several years".

"Even when their stomach disorders had become so bad that they barely ate, I had remained quietly confident that I would find the right moment to really confront them and make them see sense," she recalls. "But I now realise how hard it would have been to have entered their world once they had reached that stage of physical addiction, because I had become far less important to them than their drink."

"Looking back, I wish I had tried to involve other people before it was too late, but at the time I had felt that talking to a doctor or self-help group would somehow have constituted a betrayal of confidence. I also regret not giving up alcohol myself and setting the right example."

> 'If you're sick and tired of feeling sick and tired it's as good an indicator as any that you may have a drink problem.'

By subsequently going teetotal, even though she was never more than a moderate social drinker herself, she has no doubt that she has contributed towards a third friend overcoming their drink problem.

She says, "It seems quite surreal now to think back to the times that I enjoyed drinking with both friends who eventually died from drink, even during the last months of their lives. I was happy to tell them to stop drinking but would still drink with them, knowing that it was okay for me to do so because I didn't have an addiction problem myself."

"I drank with them primarily because they had become socially excluded, which is what eventually happens to problem drinkers, and I was determined not to exclude them from my own life. But if only I had shown some leadership during the earlier stages when their addiction was primarily psychological then maybe, just maybe, they would have realised that I was being serious about their need to change."

> 'Anyone who tells you that you are boring for not drinking has an unhealthy relationship with alcohol themselves.'

Since becoming teetotal herself 18 months ago, Lucy has become acutely conscious of the fact that some people who purported to be close friends had little in common with her other than a desire to crack a bottle of wine or two. They frequently accuse of her of being "boring" and ask when she is going to start drinking again.

"Anyone who tells you that you are boring for not drinking has an unhealthy relationship with alcohol themselves," she observes. "If only they could see how boring they are towards the end of the evening when they start repeating themselves every few minutes."

Key points

- The trick is to get the person to feel they have made their own decision to seek help

- You have effectively already lost any friend that has a serious physical addiction

- Sometimes you have to accept defeat – you are not omnipotent

- Setting the right example may at least help you to live with yourself more easily

- Regarding someone with a serious physical addiction as ill can help you detach yourself

- From now on the primary focus should be on helping yourself

- Joining Al-Anon or other self-help groups can provide a solution

Chapter 9:
Helping Employees

The fact that the majority of people with drink problems are actually in work can have implications for businesses both from a health and safety and a productivity perspective. Nevertheless, unless they are actually active in industries where safety is a critical issue, employers commonly fail to devote to the subject anything like the attention it deserves.

"Companies are invariably reluctant to admit they have alcohol problems, but having them is no more remarkable than admitting they have to provide access to toilets for their staff."

Kate McHugh, Counselling Manager Occupational Health at BUPA Wellness

Absenteeism

According to an estimate by the Health & Safety Executive (HSE), alcohol could account for up to one twentieth of all incidences of work absenteeism in the UK. A fair proportion of this absenteeism is caused by those without any kind of addiction who go out on the odd bender and feel so ill the next day that they are forced to take the day off. Nevertheless, this estimate does not include the impact of those who turn up for work slightly late because they are the worse for drink, or who come to work in a state that precludes them from making any useful contribution.

Performance and productivity

The consequences of employees being under the influence of alcohol or suffering from hangovers whilst at work are more difficult to quantify, but could in fact prove far more costly for some businesses than absenteeism.

Even a relatively junior worker could, for example, lose an important client or chalk up a significant financial loss by sending an email to the wrong person, ordering the wrong equipment or adding an additional nought to a bill. Inappropriate behaviour at office parties or other occasions when the drink is flowing can result in sexual harassment claims or damage long-term relationships with both colleagues and customers.

> "If you are trying to do any kind of paperwork and you are dehydrated your accuracy and acumen will suffer."
>
> Dr. Scott Middleton, Chiropractor (See Case Study, page 195)

Morale can also become severely dented when problem drinkers become irritable and argumentative, and when others in their team become resentful at having to carry some of their workload because their performance suffers.

Because alcohol can affect people's muscle function, stamina and ability to concentrate, anyone who gets drunk really needs to give themselves 48 hours to allow their body tissue sufficient time to recover to enable them to perform at their optimum.

Health and safety

Although there are no exact figures available with regard to the number of workplace accidents towards which excessive drinking has contributed, it is clear that alcohol can effect judgement and physical co-ordination. Drinking even small amounts before carrying out any work that is "safety sensitive" will increase the chances of an accident.

If someone drinks two pints of ordinary strength beer or half a bottle of wine at lunchtime, they will still have alcohol in their bloodstream three hours later, because the body is only able to rid itself of half a pint of normal strength beer, or its equivalent, every hour in the case of a man and every hour and a half in the case of a woman.

Even those who stay up drinking late the night before, can pose a significant safety risk when they come to work the next morning. If, for example, they went to bed at 3am after drinking eight pints of beer and arrived at work at 8am, they will still have sufficient alcohol left in the bloodstream to make it essential that they are not permitted to carry out work that involves driving, using machinery, electrical equipment or ladders, or to make decisions that could compromise the safety of others.

> **"Alcohol is probably the most dangerous psychoactive drug. It hits every part of the body and starts messing around with all the switches, meaning that people take riskier decisions. Even half a pint of beer at lunchtime can have a significant impact on behaviour."**
>
> **Kate Keenan, Chartered Occupational Psychologist**

Employers have a general duty under the Health and Safety at Work Act 1974, to ensure the health, safety and welfare of their employees. So those who knowingly allow an employee under the influence of excess alcohol to continue working in a capacity that places the employee or others at risk could be prosecuted. The employees themselves are also required to take reasonable care of themselves and others who could be affected by what they do.

In the transport industry, the misuse of alcohol is also controlled by additional legislation. The Transport and Works Act 1992, makes it a criminal offence for certain workers to be unfit through drink when they are working on railways, tramways and other guided transport systems. In the event of an offence being committed, the operators of the transport system would themselves be guilty of an offence unless they had shown all due diligence in trying to prevent the incident from occurring.

The importance of an alcohol policy

Whilst drink problems in the workplace can be difficult to tackle, especially for small firms that don't have an HR department or even a single personnel specialist, taking appropriate action in advance can greatly minimise problems that eventually come to light.

The first step, which should be taken by any company that employs even a handful of people, should be to draw up a written alcohol policy that spells out clearly exactly what employees can and cannot do with regard to drinking in the workplace. It should also make it clear that anyone who comes forward and volunteers a drink problem will receive the company's full support in helping them to try and make a recovery.

The policy may need to have more stringent rules for those working in jobs with significant health and safety risks than it does for staff involved in other capacities, but it is crucial that it is perceived to be fair. This means that senior staff must not enjoy any kind of exemption.

> "The chief executive must be prepared to sack a senior manager if they have to, and make it clear to everyone in the organisation what will happen if they break the alcohol regulations. This way no-one feels discriminated against."
>
> Dr. Joan Harvey, Chartered Psychologist

The presence of a formal policy leaves far less room for misunderstanding and, by pledging support to those who own up to problems, it helps prevent denial from problem drinkers. It can also help protect employers in the event of liability issues because, in the event of a serious alcohol-related accident, the court is likely to enquire what the company's alcohol policy is.

CASE STUDY: TREATING THEM LIKE ADULTS

When DMM Engineering decided it was essential to introduce an alcohol policy 10 years ago, its single greatest problem had been employees turning up to work with alcohol still in their system after late night drinking sessions that lasted well into the early hours.

This clearly represented a serious safety risk for the heavy engineering company, based in Llanberis, Gwynedd in North Wales. Binge drinking was the norm in this rural community, and Sunday nights experienced particularly high levels of drunkenness.

But the alcohol policy, which has been subject to only minor revisions every three years, forbids anyone to attend work if they are over the drink-driving limit. It's not policed by random testing, but anyone suspected of being over the limit is sent home by their supervisor and summoned for an interview the next day.

'The policy also bans all alcohol from the premises and prohibits lunchtime drinking – even if taking clients out to lunch.'

"We wouldn't normally be looking to prove anything or to take any disciplinary action on a first offence," explains Richard Cuthbertson, chairman of DMM Engineering. "The interview would run more along the lines of a friendly chat, enquiring whether the employee concerned has a drink problem and pointing out how dangerous their behaviour could prove."

"It states in their contract of employment that we could summarily dismiss them for being under the influence of drink, but we have never actually done so, although we might be tempted to if they are clearly putting lives at risk. It should be stressed that, like all aspects of the alcohol policy, this applies to employees of any level of seniority, including myself."

"We believe that if you treat people like adults they behave like adults, so we say that if you have to get drunk then please do it on a Friday night," he continues. "The message seems to have got across because we no longer have a problem with Sunday night drinking, but we know from anecdotal feedback that around half of our employees aged under 30 get regularly hammered on a Friday night."

'We believe that if you treat people like adults they behave like adults.'

Although it cannot actually be proven that it was as a direct result of introducing the alcohol policy, DMM Engineering hasn't had to send a single employee home for breaking the guidelines during the last three years.

The policy, drawn up with the help of the police and a local health promotion agency, also bans all alcohol from the premises and prohibits lunchtime drinking – even if taking clients out to lunch. Those socialising with clients in the evenings are, however, permitted to drink up to sensible levels.

The alcohol policy also pledges support to those who volunteer serious drink problems, and the company would be prepared to consider paying for the costs of sending an employee to a private residential rehab clinic, although it has never actually had to do so. It has, however, allowed employees time off to visit their GP and attend counselling sessions.

Straightforward example

An alcohol policy doesn't have to be long and complicated, and there is no reason why many small businesses should not simply use the sample policy below, which has been designed by the HSE.

A MODEL ALCOHOL POLICY

(As suggested by the Health and Safety Executive)

A model workplace alcohol policy would cover the following areas:

- **Aims**

    Why have a policy?

    Who does the policy apply to?

    (Note: best practice would be for the policy to apply equally to all grades of staff and types of work.)

- **Responsibility**

    Who is responsible for implementing the policy?

    (Note: all managers and supervisors will be responsible in some way but it will be more effective if a senior employee is named as having overall responsibility.)

- **The rules**

    How does the company expect employees to behave to ensure that their alcohol consumption does not have a detrimental effect on their work?

- **Special circumstances**

    Do the rules apply in all situations or are there exceptions?

- **Confidentiality**

  A statement assuring employees that any alcohol problem will be treated in strict confidence.

- **Help**

  A description of the support available to employees who have problems because of their drinking.

- **Information**

  A commitment to providing employees with general information about the effects of drinking alcohol on health and safety.

- **Disciplinary action**

  The circumstances in which disciplinary action will be taken.

Considerations in drawing up a policy

The policy must be seen as helpful as opposed to punitive, but employers with workforces of any size are most unlikely to come up with a format that meets with unanimous approval. Heavy drinkers may resent the fact that stricter conditions are being imposed, whilst those who don't drink much could either welcome having clearer guidelines or resent them on the grounds that they appear to constitute unnecessary additional bureaucracy.

The first step is to decide what level of drinking you are prepared to permit. For example, do you want to have a zero tolerance attitude that bans all alcohol from the workplace and prohibits any drinking whatsoever by staff on official duty? Or are you going to permit certain exceptions, such as when staff are entertaining clients?

Alternatively, are you going to tolerate a certain level of drinking? If so, what level? Some experts recommend the drink-driving limit (currently 80 milligrams of alcohol per 100 millilitres of blood) as being a suitable level to tolerate.

"The drink-driving limit is probably too high, but it is easy to explain. You are saying that if you are not fit to drive a car then you are not fit to do your job, which gives employees the impression that you are not trying to control their social lives but merely trying to make sure they can do their jobs the next morning."

Kate Keenan, Chartered Occupational Psychologist

Even if you take the above approach, you must still decide whether you are going to allow any drinking of alcohol actually on the premises, either during working hours or at all. Don't forget that if you ban it from the premises altogether that also means emptying out the fridges in the boardroom!

Although many companies involved in industries with an unusually high exposure to accidents do impose a complete ban on alcohol consumption whilst staff are on official duty, it is unlikely to prove terribly practical for many other kinds of organisations. Staff would, for example, be unlikely to take too kindly to not being allowed to drink at retirement parties, celebrations of business success or industry business functions held in the evenings, unless they could be persuaded that there was a very good reason for it.

Imposing a complete ban on alcohol could, in fact, be argued to constitute a change to the contract of employment and would therefore have to be discussed with a legal adviser and, if appropriate, trade unions.

'The presence of a formal policy leaves far less room for misunderstanding and, by pledging support to those who own up to problems, it helps prevent denial from problem drinkers."

The issue of how such a policy is to be policed would also need to receive serious consideration, as it may fall somewhere short of meeting with the type of "willing compliance" that is ideally required.

Imposing a complete ban with certain pre-agreed exceptions and with further exceptions that can be approved in advance by senior management is therefore likely to represent a more realistic option. But policy on grey areas, such as drinking on a train journey back from official duty, must be made crystal clear.

The potential downside of this approach, however, is that the overall policy could come across as somewhat blurred and could be open to misinterpretation. There is also the risk that some managers might impose the letter of the law more strictly than others.

Determining the level of support

Careful consideration must also be given to the actual level of support that the company will offer to those who volunteer drink problems. At one end of the scale, this could simply involve permitting the individual concerned a few days or weeks off work to visit their GP or to attend counselling sessions, together with referrals to AA or other self-help groups.

But many companies may also wish to offer a measure of financial support. Buying into an external occupational health service on an ad-hoc basis could cost no more than £1,000 to £1,500 per case (See page 187), and could be sufficient to instigate a full recovery.

Making a commitment to pay for employees with drink problems to attend a private residential rehab clinic may prove beyond the budgets of many small companies, but it is well worth considering by those organisations that can afford to. If you select the clinic carefully – and some offer discounted rates and slightly shorter stays for corporate business – the total bill is likely to be in the region of £5,000 to £12,000 (See Chapter 5, pages 99).

> **"Once you have taken into account the costs of recruitment, retraining and sick pay, it is easy to see that the costs of residential rehab could prove a good investment."**
>
> Prof. Michael O'Donnell, Chief Medical Officer at Unum

Fair but firm

Whatever level of support you provide, it should be made clear that your company's continued help depends on the employee co-operating fully with those administering the treatment and that, if they fail to do so, the employer will go down the disciplinary route.

People who are dependent on drink have a much better chance of making a recovery if they are allowed to remain in work, but that doesn't mean that employers should treat them with kid gloves. They must be made highly aware that support is available but also highly aware of the consequences of abusing that support.

CASE STUDY: SPELLING OUT THE ALCOHOL POLICY

"The key to a successful alcohol policy is clarity," explains Patrick McGrath, HR Director at Virgin Trains. "It must be totally clear what support there is for those who need help and what the consequences are if anyone breaks the rules."

"There is no point in blurring anything, because doing so just doesn't work for anyone. Employers need to spell out everything clearly and state that if employees fail with their commitment to the firm then that's it, they've blown it. Employers must then make sure that they stick to carrying out the course of action outlined for when the guidelines are broken."

> 'It must be totally clear what support there is for those who need help and what the consequences are if anyone breaks the rules.'

Every member of staff at Virgin Trains receives a copy of the company's alcohol policy when they join and are continually re-briefed every six months. The exact content of their policy will, however, vary according to the duties they will be carrying out, because "safety-critical staff", such as drivers and people in positions responsible for making decisions which can compromise safety, are subject to strict safety laws under the Transport and Works Act 1992.

Safety-critical staff are subject to random screening, with 5% to 10% of them being tested every year. The company is in fact so upfront about this stance, that even job applicants receive literature about it when they are sent their application forms, because part of the recruitment process will involve a screening.

Screening will also routinely take place after an incident and will be used if staff working in any capacity are suspected of violating the alcohol guidelines – in the case of safety-critical staff, being found to have drunk alcohol within eight hours of a shift will, for example, result in instant dismissal.

The policy also states, however, that any member of staff who comes forward and admits a drink problem will receive support, which can include being offered counselling or being referred to outsourced specialists by the occupational health department. On occasions this has even included funding inpatient stays at residential rehabilitation clinics.

> 'Success rates are quite high when employees want to do something about it, but the half-hearted attempts tend to fail.'

Those receiving treatment are required to sign a contract documenting their willingness to solve the problem, and if they don't abide by this they get dismissed.

"We try and find the right solution on a case-by-case basis," continues McGrath, "and the majority of people we help get back to work again. Success rates are quite high when employees want to do something about it, but the half-hearted attempts tend to fail."

"A number of people have been astounded by our commitment to work with them and have said years later that they are really grateful for the fact that we have changed their lives. We even get letters from partners thanking us."

The importance of communication

Having an alcohol policy is one thing, but making people aware of it is quite another. So the key is to ensure that it becomes more than just a minor component of a staff handbook handed to new recruits which gets stuffed in a drawer and forgotten about.

One way of raising awareness of the alcohol policy can be to pay for briefings on alcohol issues to be conducted in the workplace by external parties, such as business psychologists, occupational health professionals or local social services' alcohol and drug units. A key message that should be imparted is that the policy is there to help people rather than catch them out. Such external parties can also play a valuable role in educating those in managerial positions on how to spot the signs of drink problems in employees.

"It's really just a question of educating line managers and increasing their awareness of the signs and symptoms of those who may or may not be abusing alcohol."

Eugene Farrell, Business Manager, Organisational Health Management at AXA PPP healthcare

---

Some occupational health providers will do training for up to 15 managers for under £1,000 a day, and these sessions can also provide managers with a valuable opportunity to appraise their own attitudes towards alcohol. There's normally more than one person sitting with their arms folded and seeming a little reluctant to join in!

Screening

But whilst experts on alcoholism in the workplace commonly emphasise that expenditure on such an educational function tends to be money well spent, they advise employers who are not working in safety-sensitive industries not to pay for the considerable costs of random alcohol screening of staff.

Screening is a sensitive issue and the prior agreement of the workforce to it is essential because of the practical and legal issues involved. The practice is only likely to be considered acceptable if it is clearly designed to prevent risks to others and is seen to represent part of a company's overall occupational health policy.

> "Don't have random screenings unless you have a known problem, because it tells staff you don't trust them. Most people use them to try and catch one person, but if you suspect someone is drinking you need to tackle them on performance."
>
> Kate Keenan, Chartered Occupational Psychologist

If screening is considered essential, however, the agreement of its principle must be incorporated into every member of staff's contract of employment. Whilst this may be a reasonably straightforward thing to do for new staff, there could be a problem with existing staff, because they are under no legal obligation to agree to changes in their terms and conditions of employment. They could therefore resign and claim unfair dismissal if the employer tried to force a test on them against their wishes.

The written consent of each individual must also be obtained for each test, and medical confidentiality must also be assured. You would not, for example, be able to tell an employee's line manager that they had liver damage. You would only be allowed to say whether they were fit or unfit for work.

Other safeguards

Offering employees a subsidised gym membership or encouraging a sandwich culture at lunchtime can help to reduce the chances of drink problems developing, as it makes people less likely to go out and have a drink. For larger companies, setting up an employee assistance programme (EAP) to offer telephone counselling backed up with the ability to receive face-to-face counselling, can also provide a valuable safeguard.

> **"There is ample evidence from the US that EAPs work in helping to combat drink problems."**
>
> Dr. Joan Harvey, Chartered Psychologist

EAPs actually originated as a way of combating alcohol and drug abuse in the US, and they can be particularly useful for helping employees exploring the issues underlying their drink problems. Employees can phone them as often as they like, although face-to-face meetings are likely to be limited to between five and eight sessions.

Many EAP providers will be unwilling to take on schemes with under 50 members and, although some might do schemes as small as 20, these will arguably not represent as good overall value to employers. As well as helping employees, EAPs are highly valued for their ability to feedback anonymous management-related information to employers. But for schemes of under 50 members, confidentiality issues would ensure that this management information would be of a very low level.

The costs of setting up an EAP will depend primarily on the size of the scheme concerned. A scheme for 50 members may cost around £40 per head per year, but this cost is likely to reduce to around £15 per head for 1,000 members and to around £5 per head for 100,000 members.

Facing the music

The key to employers dealing with drink problems in the workplace is to avoid trying to do too much themselves and to refer the individuals concerned to suitably qualified professionals. An employee with a drink problem is far more likely to feel comfortable discussing it with an occupational health specialist than with a line manager or other colleague.

> "Nobody ever started out their career with the ambition of becoming a drunk, so something has gone wrong with their lives and occupational health people are best placed to find out what it is and to help sort it out. They tend to be very successful as they are not judgemental, which managers can be."
>
> Kate Keenan, Chartered Occupational Psychologist

More often than not, the drinking is the symptom of further underlying problems that could result from the workplace or from outside it, and is in fact quite often a combination of both – involving anything from excessive work pressure and concerns about job security, to relationships in the home and relationships with line managers.

Spirals can easily develop in which a number of different factors start feeding off each other. For example, lack of job satisfaction or an excessive workload can take its toll on an employee's marriage, which can in turn detract from their performance at work.

> "In quite a large number of cases, a drink problem might signify stress-related problems. So you should try and deal with the underlying sources of the problem. It could be one of a number of work or non-work related issues."
>
> Prof. Cary Cooper, Professor of Organisational Psychology and Health at Lancaster University Management School

So it is important not to make assumptions about people or to write them off. Remember what they were like before they had the problem and try and help them recover.

Using external services

There isn't necessarily any need for a firm to spend heavily on having its own in–house occupational health department, because it is quite possible to buy into external occupational health services on an ad-hoc basis relatively inexpensively.

Some occupational health providers are quite prepared to help small organisations who approach them out of the blue with one-off cases (For contact details see Appendix 3, page 270). Sending an employee for an initial assessment may cost around £150 and even if a dozen subsequent counselling sessions also prove to be needed – which should be sufficient in most cases – their combined cost is likely to be in the region of £1,000.

> "Employees with drink problems are likely to represent some of the most difficult cases you will ever deal with, so the message is to get as much help as you can. If you have an occupational health service make sure you use it, and if you don't have one there are many external services you can buy into."
>
> Dr. Olivia Carlton, former Registrar of the Faculty of Occupational Medicine

Most EAP providers (For contact details see Appendix 3, page 269) are also willing to allow their services to be bought into on a pay-as-you go basis by firms who don't have their own in-house schemes. Both the telephone-based and face-to-face counselling services these offer can be useful for tackling underlying mental health issues that have not as yet become absenteeism problems, avoiding the need for lengthy waits on the NHS. £1,000 to £1,500 is likely to cover the costs of an initial assessment and any subsequent counselling sessions considered necessary.

> "Referring employees to EAPs might help to get at the source of the underlying problem for the individual, but EAPs do not necessarily deal with the underlying structural problems in the organisation or its culture."
>
> Prof. Cary Cooper, Professor of Organisational Psychology and Health at Lancaster University Management School

The cost of recruiting and training a replacement may be greater than the cost of paying for such treatment but, if you are not prepared to invest any company money in treatment, you should at least be encouraging the employee to seek help from their GP, a local State-funded alcohol advisory service, or a self-help group or helpline service like FRANK or Drinkline (See Chapter 1, page 11).

There is also much to be said for finding out how other local businesses are dealing with drink problems by contacting local business forums, and for establishing personal contact with your local State-funded alcohol advisory service – as this could make things easier if you experience a drink problem with an employee in the future.

Occupational health specialists can carry out liver function tests, provide one-to-one counselling, encourage attendance of self-help groups and – if a problem is very severe – consider whether the individual concerned is likely to benefit from residential rehab.

Spotting the symptoms

But success with referral to either internal or external professional help inevitably depends primarily on the ability to spot the relevant symptoms. Many of the telltale signs of employee drink problems trotted out by occupational health experts hardly constitute rocket science (See below).

THE TELLTALE SIGNS

- Consistently late for work on Mondays.

- Often disappearing early on Fridays – especially when they have received their monthly pay cheque.

- Poor time keeping generally / early departures from the workplace.

- Many sick notes with gastritis.

- Drop in performance / frequent mistakes in work / missed deadlines / concentration difficulties / decline in reliability.

- Irritability / poor relationships with colleagues.

- Becoming involved in more accidents.

- Dishevelled appearance / alcohol on breath.

But many of these symptoms also relate to other conditions, particularly depression. So being able to spot drink problems in the workplace often boils down to how well you know your staff.

> "Nothing can replace the knowledge a line manager has of their employees, and this knowledge can enable the manager to spot changes from a very early stage."
>
> Kate McHugh, Counselling Manager Occupational Health at BUPA Wellness

Making the approach

The initial approach used in raising the issue with a suspected problem drinker should embody the same "supportive but firm" ethos outlined in the company's alcohol policy (see page 176).

Never broach the subject when they are actually drunk, and only do so after gathering some initial evidence based on studying the individual's behaviour. The exact approach to be used will obviously depend on the particular circumstances but, without being confrontational, you need to get across the message that you realise that something isn't right.

> "They've got to know that you know, but you must be fair and kind. Ask them what you can do to help."
>
> Dr. Joan Harvey, Occupational Psychologist

If it's one of the directors, it may be best for HR to have a quiet word. But, if it's a less senior member of staff who has a good relationship with their line manager, a friendly informal chat along the lines of "We go back a long way but I've noticed performance has dipped a bit on Mondays" could result in the employee volunteering that they have a drink problem.

Spelling out the alternatives

On being informed of suspicions that they could have a drink problem, the employee must be made aware that they have two options open to them. They can either ask for help, in which case the company will act towards them in a highly supportive fashion, or, if they continue to deny what is obviously a genuine problem, it should be made clear that the issue will be dealt with via the disciplinary route. Try not to be judgemental or threatening but at the same time try to be direct and to avoid skirting around the issue.

> **"Never send an employee to occupational health without discussing the matter with the individual concerned first."**
>
> Dr. Olivia Carlton, former Registrar of the Faculty of Occupational Medicine

Even employees who admit to a drink problem should initially have it spelt out to them that failure to co-operate fully with occupational health, or any other professional help assigned, will result in disciplinary action.

Don't delay

Any delays in raising drink problem issues with employees are only likely to make matters worse. Indeed, occupational health professionals report cases of individuals dying within weeks of being referred as a result of already suffering from advanced liver damage. Also, don't forget the impact that someone with a deteriorating drink problem could have on the rest of the workforce.

"If you can see there is a problem, don't let it go too far. That person could not only become more ill but their drunken behaviour could have a detrimental effect on a whole range of other people, from colleagues to customers/clients and suppliers."

Prof. Cary Cooper, Professor of Organisational Psychology and Health at Lancaster University Management School

Those in recovery make good workers

The good news is that many employees with drink problems are able, in time, to regain full control over their lives and return to their previous work performance level. Indeed, experts commonly agree that those that have conquered drink problems are likely to represent exceptionally valuable assets to any workforce.

"In my experience, the chances of curing a drink problem at work are quite high if you are supportive. You are probably talking about success rates of somewhere between a third and a half, and once former drinkers have been on the wagon for a year or more they are actually less at risk of dependency than their standard colleagues."

Prof. Michael O'Donnell, Chief Medical Officer at Unum

"People go back and drive planes and trains and cars after being in rehab, and I can tell you from my experience that they are much safer than their colleagues who are still failing to address their issues with alcohol."

Kate McHugh, Counselling Manager Occupational Health at BUPA Wellness

"If they work with occupational health and come good they often think it's the best thing that has happened to them. This makes them better workers, much more loyal to the firm because it has helped them, and likely to advise others with drink problems to seek help."

Kate Keenan, Chartered Occupational Psychologist

"Unlike virtually any other condition I've worked with as a psychologist, you can see the most dramatic transformation in people, who can discover extraordinary potential they didn't know they had."

Nick Barton, Joint Chief Executive of Action on Addiction

"The recovering addict is so grateful to be in recovery and to have regained their life that they rarely take a day off work. They become very conscientious and highly valued members of the team, enjoying life and people and demonstrating a new vigour that is often infectious."

Keith Burns, Managing Director of independent advice and referral agency ADMIT Services

"If you are in genuine recovery the enlightened employer will know you are likely to make a very good employee."

Dr. Olivia Carlton, former Registrar of the Faculty of Occupational Medicine

Areas of less agreement

But there is less agreement amongst experts with regard to whether employers should insist that employees who successfully complete treatment should never touch another drop or permit them to continue drinking in moderation. When the former approach is taken, opinions also differ with regard to whether employees who relapse should be given another chance.

In both cases, there is much to be said for employers using their judgement and treating each case on its own merits, as opposed to setting ground rules in stone. As we have frequently discussed in earlier chapters, there is a big difference between whether someone has had a psychological or a physical addiction. There is also a significant difference between someone who starts drinking again within weeks and someone who does so six months later in response to a specific setback or simply because they are curious to see if they are now able to drink in moderation again.

"I used to feel employers shouldn't give a second chance, but it's important to understand that employees who have gone dry may want to experiment to see if it's a problem any longer. So I would recommend giving them one chance to fall off the wagon."

Prof. Michael O'Donnell, Chief Medical Officer at Unum

CASE STUDY: CHIROPRACTOR KEEPS CLEAR HEAD

Dr. Scott Middleton pinpoints his fifth year at chiropractic college, when he actually started treating patients in clinics, as being the crucial turning point in his attitude towards drink.

"Prior to that, I had only ever drunk for social reasons, but I thought nothing of having on-draft lager and bitter at the flat I shared with my fellow students," he recalls. "I was quite happy to have a couple of pints any night of the week, which was never enough to give me a hangover although, like most students, I also enjoyed the occasional binge at parties."

"But since I started clinical work I have adopted a rule that I never drink the night before. Although if I do not have an early clinic the following morning I am now occasionally prepared to allow myself a couple of glasses of wine with my evening meal."

'In my view, large companies could do far more to increase productivity by attempting to educate employees in the dangers of drinking.'

Dr. Middleton, who is now 55 and has two chiropractic practices in the Manchester/Cheshire area, normally only drinks on Friday and Saturday evenings and, even then, he never has more than two – or possibly three – small glasses of wine. This contrasts notably with when he is on holiday, when he thinks nothing of having half a bottle of wine at lunchtime followed by a full bottle in the evening most days.

"As someone who has trained in medical science, I am only too aware that the after-effects of alcohol can lower a person's clinical acumen," he continues. "If you don't think clearly you can miss the nuance in someone's voice, which could easily lead to a misdiagnosis and could possibly prove fatal."

"I often have to almost 'drag' information out of people by asking them questions from imaginary boxes in my mind, and if I was even slightly the worse for drink I could miss some of those boxes. This could, for example, result in me failing to spot something as important as a tumour, and I diagnose about one of these a month."

Dr. Middleton also mentions that he treats a lot of well-known footballers and athletes and would be very hard pressed to name one that ever drinks the night before performing. This is because alcohol dehydrates the body – including the brain – and research has shown that those who are dehydrated perform less well.

> 'If you are trying to do any kind of paperwork and you are dehydrated your accuracy and acumen will suffer.'

"Logically it will be the same for any job, whether it requires physical or mental abilities" he argues. "If you are trying to do any kind of paperwork and you are dehydrated your accuracy and acumen will suffer. In my view, large companies could do far more to increase productivity by attempting to educate employees in the dangers of drinking both excess alcohol and of drinking alcohol at inappropriate times."

"Some people are prepared to work all hours to try and advance themselves, but they don't pay enough attention to the importance of being able to concentrate with a clear mind. They would be much better off confining their drinking to weekends and holidays."

Key points

- Even half a pint of beer at lunchtime can have a significant impact on performance

- A written alcohol policy should make it clear exactly what employees can and can't do

- It should also detail the support available to those who admit to drink problems

- The consequences of abusing that support must also be spelt out

- Don't have random screenings unless you have a known problem

- Employees who defeat drink problems often make exceptionally good workers

- Occupational health services and access to EAPs can be bought on a pay-as-you-go basis

Appendices

Appendix 1:
More Detailed Medical Information

What exactly is alcohol?

Alcohol is a drug derived from the fermentation of sugar by yeast. Its main psychoactive ingredient is ethanol, which dissolves quickly in water and is easily absorbed into the bloodstream. In small doses, it acts on receptors in the brain to make people feel uninhibited and provides a general sense of well-being. But drinking more alcohol starts to affect the balance and the speech centres of the brain and is likely to have a depressant effect. The brain's receptors adapt to alcohol when it is consumed regularly, meaning that higher doses are needed to cause the same effect.

Excessive alcohol consumption can lead to dehydration, low blood sugar and poisoning – i.e. 'a hangover'. The dehydration occurs because alcohol stimulates urination, and the low blood sugar because it stimulates the production of insulin. All alcoholic drinks also contain impurities known as 'congeners', which contribute to the poisoning effect. Less than 10% of alcohol is eliminated from the body in urine, breath and sweat. The rest combines with oxygen in the blood to release heat, energy or calories.

How much is it safe to drink?

- Men should drink no more than 21 units of alcohol a week (and no more than 3 or 4 units in one day).

- Women should drink no more than 14 units of alcohol a week (and no more than 2 or 3 units in any one day).

- One small (125ml) glass of wine (12% abv) is 1.5 units.

- One standard pub measure of fortified wine, like sherry or port, is 1 unit.

- A shot of tequila/sambuca etc. (25ml) is 1 unit.

- A single pub measure of gin, vodka, rum or whisky (25ml) is 1 unit but some measures are 35ml or 50ml.

- Half a pint of standard beer or lager (3.5% abv) is 1 unit.

- Half a pint of regular cider (5% abv) is 1.4 units.

What matters is the total amount of alcohol you consume, as measured by units, and not the type of drink you are downing. If you are drinking only beer and wine, you can cause yourself just as much harm as if you are drinking spirits.

Additionally, when taking account of these recommended drinking guidelines, it is also important to realise that many commonly drunk beers are stronger than a "standard beer or lager". Stella and Kronenberg, for example, are in the region of 5% abv (alcohol by volume). It is also important to realise that wine glasses have increased in size and that a glass of wine you consume when you are out may well contain around 3 units of alcohol.

What harm does alcohol cause the liver?

A healthy liver should contain little or no fat but, when the liver breaks down alcohol, it stores the fat, and too much of it creates a condition known as fatty liver. Your liver can recover from fatty liver and return to normal if you revert to drinking within sensible limits, but if you carry on drinking to excess you can cause more serious damage. In fact, you will have a one in three chance of developing alcoholic hepatitis, which will involve your liver becoming puffy, swollen and tender.

This could happen quite suddenly after a weekend of binge drinking and could even kill you. Most people can recover from alcoholic hepatitis if they stop drinking completely – cutting down only reduces the amount of damage done. But people who need to be admitted to hospital with severe alcoholic hepatitis have around a one in three chance of dying within the first month.

The final stage of alcoholic liver disease is cirrhosis, which involves the liver becoming hardened and scarred and running out of healthy cells to support its normal functions. This can lead to complete liver failure. Your liver cannot recover from cirrhosis, but you can prevent further damage and increase your chances of survival if you stop drinking. If your liver is badly affected by cirrhosis and you continue to drink, it is estimated that you have only a one in three chance of living for five years. But if you stop drinking you can almost double your chances of survival.

Who is most likely to suffer liver damage?

Everyone reacts to alcohol in different ways, but research shows the following groups may be most at risk:

- People who inherit genes that don't allow proper metabolism of alcohol.

- Overweight people.

- Women – partly because of their smaller body size and build, they have a higher proportion of body fat than men to absorb alcohol and they produce fewer of the enzymes that break down and remove alcohol.

Vague symptoms of alcoholic liver damage

If you have alcoholic liver damage you may have vague symptoms such as:

- Feeling some pain at the lower righthand side of your ribs.

- Feeling tired and generally unwell.

- Loss of appetite.

- A sick nauseous feeling, particularly in the mornings, and often accompanied by diarrhoea.

Specific symptoms of alcoholic liver damage

Speak to your doctor at once if you have any of the following symptoms:

- Yellow eyes or, in more severe cases, yellow skin.
- Vomiting blood.
- Dark, black tarry stools.
- Significant weight loss.
- Periods of confusion or poor memory.
- Swelling of the stomach area and legs.
- Fever – possibly with shivering attacks.
- Itching.

What harm does alcohol cause to the rest of your body?

Excessive consumption of alcohol is capable of causing around 100 different medical conditions. It can, for example, lead to or increase the likelihood of suffering from:

- Vomiting and passing out.
- Stomach disorders.
- Malnutrition.
- Pancreatitis, leading to diabetes.
- High blood pressure.
- Heart problems, including heart attacks.
- Strokes.
- Anaemia.

- Vitamin deficiencies.

- Chest infections.

- Sexual difficulties, including impotence.

- Depression, anxiety.

- Decreased mental functioning.

- Brain disease caused by vitamin B deficiency.

- Osteoporosis.

- Problems with nerves in the arms and legs.

- Cancer of the liver, mouth, throat, neck, bowel and breast.

- Gout.

- Swelling, muscle weakness and tissue damage.

- Bleeding from the arteries in the abdomen.

- Skin diseases, including psoriasis, eczema, acne, and rashes.

- Hormonal problems.

- Reduction in fertility.

- Gum disease and tooth decay.

- Psychosis – long-term drinkers can start to hear voices.

- Damage to unborn babies in pregnant women.

- Accidents and violence.

- Suicide.

How do you tell if you have a drink problem?

If the realisation that you regularly drink in excess of the governmental guidelines outlined on page 202 is not sufficient to convince you that you have a drink problem, then you may wish to try the following tests that are often used by medical experts.

A. The CAGE Questionnaire

1. Have you ever felt you should Cut down on your drinking?

2. Have people Annoyed you by criticising your drinking?

3. Have you ever felt bad or Guilty about your drinking?

4. Have you ever had an Eye opener – a drink first thing in the morning to steady your nerves or get rid of a hangover?

Scoring the CAGE questionnaire

The answers to the questions are scored 0 for "no" and 1 for "yes".

If you have a score of 2 or greater it is indicative that you have a drink problem.

B. The Fast Alcohol Screening Test (FAST)

For the following questions please circle the answer which best applies.

1 drink = 1/2 a pint of beer or 1 glass of wine or 1 single spirits

1. MEN: How often do you have EIGHT or more drinks on one occasion?
   WOMEN: How often do you have SIX or more drinks on one occasion?

   (0) – Never
   (1) – Less than monthly
   (2) – Monthly
   (3) – Weekly
   (4) – Daily or almost daily

2. How often during the last year have you been unable to remember what happened the night before because you had been drinking?

   (0) – Never
   (1) – Less than monthly
   (2) – Monthly
   (3) – Weekly
   (4) – Daily or almost daily

3. How often during the last year have you failed to do what was normally expected of you because of drinking?

(0) – Never
(1) – Less than monthly
(2) – Monthly
(3) – Weekly
(4) – Daily or almost daily

4. In the last year has a relative, friend, doctor or other health worker been concerned about your drinking or suggested you cut down?

(0) – Never
(2) – Yes, on one occasion
(4) – Yes, on more than one occasion

Scoring the FAST questionnaire

STAGE 1 – only involves question 1

If your response is "Weekly" or "Daily or almost daily" then you are a hazardous harmful or dependent drinker.

STAGE 2

Only consider questions 2, 3 and 4 if the response to question 1 is "Less than monthly" or "Monthly".

Then add together the figures above your answers for each of the four questions. If your total score for all questions combined is 3 or more you are misusing alcohol.

C. The Alcohol Use Disorders Identification Test (AUDIT)

1. How often do you have a drink containing alcohol?

   (0) – Never
   (1) – Monthly
   (2) – 2-4 times a month
   (3) – 2-3 times a week
   (4) – 4 or more times a week

2. How many units of alcohol do you drink on a typical day when you are drinking?

   (0) – 1 or 2
   (1) – 3 or 4
   (2) – 5 or 6
   (3) – 7, 8 or 9
   (4) – 10 or more

3. How often do you have six or more units of alcohol on one occasion?

   (0) – Never
   (1) – Less than monthly
   (2) – Monthly
   (3) – Weekly
   (4) – Daily or almost daily

4. How often during the last year have you found that you were not able to stop drinking once you had started?

(0) – Never
(1) – Less than monthly
(2) – Monthly
(3) – Weekly
(4) – Daily or almost daily

5. How often during the last year have you failed to do what was normally expected of you because of drinking?

(0) – Never
(1) – Less than monthly
(2) – Monthly
(3) – Weekly
(4) – Daily or almost daily

6. How often during the last year have you needed a drink first thing in the morning to get yourself going after a heavy drinking session?

(0) – Never
(1) – Less than monthly
(2) – Monthly
(3) – Weekly
(4) – Daily or almost daily

7. How often during the last year have you had a feeling of guilt or remorse after drinking?

(0) – Never
(1) – Less than monthly
(2) – Monthly
(3) – Weekly
(4) – Daily or almost daily

8. How often during the last year have you been unable to remember what happened the night before because you had been drinking?

(0) – Never
(1) – Less than monthly
(2) – Monthly
(3) – Weekly
(4) – Daily or almost daily

9. Have you or someone else been injured as a result of your drinking?

(0) – No
(2) – Yes, but not in the last year
(3) – Yes, during the last year

10. Has a relative or friend or doctor or another health worker been concerned about your drinking or suggested you cut down?

(0) – No
(2) – Yes, but not in the last year
(3) – Yes, during the last year

Scoring the AUDIT Questionnaire

Add up the figures in the left hand bracket, and if your total is greater than 8 you may have a problem with alcohol.

Appendix 2:
Recent Statistics

ALCOHOL CONSUMPTION / MISUSE

- 38% of men and 16% of women (aged 16-64) have an alcohol use disorder (26% overall), which is equivalent to approximately 8.2 million people in England.

The Alcohol Needs Assessment Research Project (Department of Health – The 2004 national alcohol needs assessment for England)

- In terms of the amount of alcohol drunk, the average weekly consumption of those who drank in the last seven days increased from 5.3 units in 1990 to 11.4 units in 2006.

Institute of Alcohol Studies

- In England in 2005, 73% of men and 58% of women reported drinking an alcoholic drink on at least one day in the week prior to interview. 13% of men and 8% of women reported drinking on every day in the previous week.

Statistics on Alcohol: England, 2007 (NHS – The Information Centre for health and social care)

- 34% of men and 20% of women had drunk more than the recommended number of units on at least one day of the week prior to interview. 18% of men and 8% of women had drunk more than twice the recommended daily intake.

  Statistics on Alcohol: England, 2007 (NHS – The Information Centre for health and social care)

- Older people were more likely to drink regularly – 28% of men and 18% of women aged 45-64 drank on five or more days in the week prior to interview, compared to 10% of men and 5% of women aged 16-24. Younger people were more likely to drink heavily, with 42% of men and 36% of women aged 16-24 drinking above the daily recommendations, compared to 16% of men and 4% of women aged 65 and over.

  Statistics on Alcohol: England, 2007 (NHS – The Information Centre for health and social care)

- In the United Kingdom, the volume of pure alcohol released for home consumption per person aged 16 and over has increased from 9.4 litres in 1993/94 to 11.4 litres in 2005/6.

  Statistics on Alcohol: England, 2007 (NHS – The Information Centre for health and social care)

- 21% of men and 9% of women are binge drinkers.

  The Alcohol Needs Assessment Research Project (Department of Health – The 2004 national alcohol needs assessment for England)

- Among men, 24% reported drinking on average more than 21 units a week. For women, 13% reported drinking more than 14 units in an average week.

  Statistics on Alcohol: England, 2007 (NHS – The Information Centre for health and social care)

- There is considerable regional variation in the levels of alcohol-related need. The prevalence of hazardous/harmful drinking varied across the regions from 18% to 29%, whilst alcohol dependence varied between regions ranging from 1.6% to 5.2%.

The Alcohol Needs Assessment Research Project (Department of Health – The 2004 national alcohol needs assessment for England)

- The prevalence of alcohol dependence overall was 3.6%, with 6% of men and 2% of women meeting these criteria nationally. This equates to 1.1 million people with alcohol dependence nationally.

The Alcohol Needs Assessment Research Project (Department of Health – The 2004 national alcohol needs assessment for England)

COST/TREATMENT

- In 2006, alcohol was 65% more affordable in the United Kingdom than it was in 1980.

Statistics on Alcohol: England, 2007 (NHS - The Information Centre for health and social care)

- Alcohol currently costs the NHS up to £1.7 billion a year.

Alcohol Concern

- Alcohol misuse has a high impact on health and social care systems, where major savings can be made. Drinking also places costs on the criminal justice system, especially with regard to public order. Overall, for every £1 spent on treatment, £5 is saved elsewhere.

Review of the Effectiveness of Treatment for Alcohol Problems (NHS National Treatment Agency for Substance Misuse)

- There are major regional variations in treatment. In the North East, only 1 in 102 people who need treatment are able to access it. This compares with a dismal national average of 1 in 18.

Alcohol Concern

- At peak times, up to 70% of all admissions to Accident and Emergency units are related to alcohol consumption.

British Liver Trust

- 35,570 NHS hospital admissions for adults in England during 2005/2006 involved mental and behavioural disorders due to alcohol consumption as the primary diagnosis, and 13,720 admissions involved alcoholic liver disease being recorded as the primary diagnosis.

Statistics on Alcohol: England, 2007 (NHS – The Information Centre for health and social care)

- Each year, alcohol takes up £0.5 billion of the national A&E budget.

Alcohol Concern

- Each year in the UK, 150,000 people are admitted to hospital and 22,000 people die prematurely due to alcohol-related causes. That death toll works out at 400 people per day. The cost to society has been estimated at over £20 billion.

British Liver Trust

- In 2005/2006, there were 52,270 NHS hospital admissions of adults in England aged 16 and over with a primary diagnosis specifically related to alcohol. This number has risen from 34,660 in 1995/1996. 70% of admissions with a primary diagnosis relating to alcohol were male.

Statistics on Alcohol: England, 2007 (NHS - The Information Centre for health and social care)

IMPACT ON HEALTH

- Alcohol intoxication and binge drinking increase the risk of acute haemorrhagic and ischemic strokes by up to ten fold.

Institute of Alcohol Studies

- Since 1991, the rate of people dying from chronic conditions linked to alcohol misuse in Britain has almost doubled.

Alcohol Concern

- In 2005, 6,570 people in England and Wales died from causes directly linked to alcohol consumption. Of these, just under two thirds (4,160) died from alcoholic liver disease. 67% of those dying from alcoholic liver disease were men.

Statistics on Alcohol: England, 2007 (NHS – The Information Centre for health and social care)

- 1 in 30 cancer deaths are attributable to alcohol misuse.

Alcohol Concern

- 5-7% of cases of hypertension are the result of heavy drinking, which makes alcohol the most prevalent cause, save for obesity.

  Alcohol Concern

- Psychiatric co-morbidity is common among problem drinkers – up to 10% for severe mental illness, up to 50% for personality disorders and up to 80% for neurotic disorders.

  Review of the Effectiveness of Treatment for Alcohol Problems (NHS National Treatment Agency for Substance Misuse)

- Alcohol misuse is related to at least 10% of the chronic disease burden.

  Alcohol Concern

- It is feared that the increase in binge drinking among young women will lead to a significant increase in breast cancer in the next half century. Most at risk are the increasing number of young binge drinkers who have four or more drinks on a night out. Their risk of breast cancer is estimated to increase by 40%.

  Institute of Alcohol Studies

- The official estimate of the number of suicides linked to alcohol misuse puts it somewhere in the range between 16% and 41%.

  Alcohol Concern

CRIME

- A minimum of 1 in 5 people arrested by police test positive for alcohol.

Institute of Alcohol Studies

- For both men and women, nearly half of the fatal assaults of which they are victims involved alcohol.

Alcohol Concern

- Up to 1,000 young people a week suffer serious facial injuries as a result of drunken assaults. 18,000 young people are scarred for life each year.

Institute of Alcohol Studies

- 32% of convicted offenders felt that their violent behaviour was related to their alcohol use.

Alcohol Concern

- An All Party Group of MPs investigating alcohol and crime was advised by the British Medical Association that alcohol is a factor in 60% to 70% of homicides, 75% of stabbings, 70% of beatings, 50% of fights and domestic assaults.

Institute of Alcohol Studies

ACCIDENTS

- Estimates of the proportion of deaths that occur in people who have been drinking range from 35% to 63% for falls, to 21% to 47% for drownings, and 12% to 61% for burns.

Institute of Alcohol Studies

- Alcohol figures in 30% of all fatal car accidents where men are the victims.

Alcohol Concern

- A conservative estimate is that alcohol is a casual factor in around 10% of fatalities from home accidents, in which case there are approximately 400 alcohol-related deaths from home accidents each year.

Institute of Alcohol Studies

WORKPLACE

- Drinking 7+ (for women) or 14+ (for men) units per week raises the likelihood of absence from work through injury by 20%. Combined with the inability to work through unemployment and early retirement and premature deaths amongst economically active people, there is a total alcohol-related output loss to the UK economy of up to £6.4 billion.

Institute of Alcohol Studies

- In many workplaces, 20% to 25% of accidents at work involve intoxicated people injuring themselves and innocent victims.

International Labour Organisation

- Those working in managerial or professional employment were most likely to report having drunk during the week prior to interview (73%) compared to those working in routine or manual positions who were less likely to report this (57%). The same pattern is seen among those reporting drinking on five or more days in the previous week, with 22% of managers and professionals reporting this compared to 13% of routine and manual workers.

Statistics on Alcohol: England, 2007 (NHS – The Information Centre for health and social care)

CHILDREN

- In 2006, 21% of pupils in England aged 11-15 reported drinking alcohol in the week prior to interview.

Statistics on Alcohol: England, 2007 (NHS – The Information Centre for healthy and social care)

- Among pupils who had drunk alcohol in the week prior to interview, the average weekly consumption almost doubled from 5.3 units in 1990 to 10.4 units in 2000. Weekly consumption has since fluctuated around this level and in 2006 was estimated at 11.4 units. However, consumption among children aged 11-13 has continued to increase, from 5.6 units in 2001 to 10.1 units in 2006.

Statistics on Alcohol: England, 2007 (NHS – The Information Centre for health and social care

- In 2005/2006, in children under 16, there were 4,060 NHS hospital admissions with a primary diagnosis specifically related to alcohol. This shows an overall increase of 29% from 3,150 in 1995/1996. Among those aged under 16, 59% of admissions with primary diagnosis relating to alcohol were girls.

Statistics on Alcohol: England, 2007 (NHS – The Information Centre for health and social care)

Appendix 3:
Sources Of Help And
Contact Details

---

1. SPECIALIST INTERMEDIARIES

• ADMIT SERVICES

Location:
London, Kent, Oxford, Cheltenham, and The Midlands, but provides a national internet/email/telephone-based service.

Website:
www.admitservices.co.uk

Type of organisation:
Fully independent alcohol detox/rehab advisory service.

Services available to:
All those seeking private detox and rehab services or a private home detox.

Contact details:
Tel: 0845 3020404
Email: keithadmit@aol.com or louiseadmit@googlemail.com

Postal address:
> Draycott House
> Cumberland Avenue
> Wellingore
> Lincoln
> LN5 0BL

Brief description of services offered:

Free independent advice from experienced addiction specialists on alcohol detox and rehab clinics in the UK and overseas. A specialist addiction doctor and counsellors are also available if required.

Unusual features:

Advice is entirely independent and it has access to a large number of clinics that other referral agencies cannot refer to. It is able to obtain substantial discounts at certain clinics. Male and female advisors are available.

Costs:

Clinics cost from £350 per week up to £10,000 per week. You do not pay for advice, as ADMIT Services receives a commission from the clinics. You do not pay any more, and usually you will pay a lot less.

Types of consumers most popular with:

Those with at least £2,000 to spend on treatment.

- ## DRYOUTNOW.COM

Location:
UK-wide.

Website:
www.DryOutNow.com

Type of organisation:
Alcohol treatment planning and advice service.

Services available to:
People with drinking problems, their friends and relatives, professionals working in the field.

Contact details:
Tel: 0845 230 8060
Email: dg@dryoutnow.com

Postal address:
DryOutNow.com
10 Harley Street
London
W1 9PF

Brief description of services offered:
Completely free, highly practical, expert advice. Telephone advice is provided by doctors and other healthcare professionals. Working with a network of professional treatment providers (counsellors, doctors, nurses and residential rehabilitation centres) throughout the UK and abroad, it provides best-value treatment of the kind best suited to the individual.

Unusual features:
Meaningful, practical advice (including all relevant contact details), is provided to all callers, whether they are seeking treatment privately, or in the NHS, or through local support groups such as Alcoholics Anonymous. Self-help books, professional treatment guidelines, self-assessment tools, contact

details of local help services, and daily news on the latest treatment innovations are available free from its website.

Costs:

All telephone advice services are provided free-of-charge. Individuals accessing private residential treatment are guaranteed to pay no more than by accessing treatment directly with one of its partner treatment providers, and in some cases pay less.

• RE-COVER

Location:
London, but provides a national service.

Website:
www.re-cover.org.uk

Type of organisation:
Addictions advice and referral company.

Services available to:
Anyone and everyone.

Contact details:
Tel: 0845 603 6530
Email: info@re-cover.org.uk

Brief description of services offered:
Re-cover provides free, unbiased, independent, confidential advice on private alcohol residential rehabilitation treatment centres in the UK, Europe and South Africa. It assesses and monitors the majority of the private rehab centres in the UK, Ireland, Spain and South Africa. It can recommend the best treatment at the best price.

Unusual features:
Everyone at Re-cover has experienced first hand the destruction alcohol addiction can have on one's life and the lives of family members. It does not enter into any exclusive arrangements with any centre or clinic either in the UK or abroad, and provides free, confidential advice on how to receive local NHS treatment as well as information on voluntary services in your area.

Costs:
There is no charge for its service, which is funded by a small referral fee paid by the treatment centre. Discounts are arranged on a person-by-person basis.

Types of consumers most popular with:
Re-cover assists people of all ages and backgrounds. Its clients are from all over the United Kingdom and Ireland.

2. REHAB CLINICS, HOSPITALS, CHARITIES & VOLUNTARY ORGANISATIONS

• BROADWAY LODGE

Location:
Weston-super-Mare, Somerset.

Website:
www.broadwaylodge.org.uk

Type of organisation:
Non-profit making rehabilitation centre, and a registered charity.

Services available to:
Both State-funded and private residents. Also has own charitable funds.

Contact details for admission:
Tel: 01934 815515
Fax: 01934 815381
Email: Admissions@broadwaylodge.org.uk

Postal address:
Contracts, Assessments & Admissions
Broadway Lodge
Oldmixon Road
Weston-super-Mare
Somerset
BS24 9NN

Brief description of facilities/courses:
33-bed residential centre providing Primary Care (lasting c8 weeks) and 22 places in adjacent building for secondary care (c13 weeks). Uses combination of 12 Step approach and motivational techniques. (See Case Study, Chapter 5, page 97.) Facilities include residential treatment, a detox programme,

aftercare, a family programme (3 days residential), a renewal programme (5 days residential), and a series of day programmes.

Unusual features:
Located in the peaceful setting of a country house. Offers alternative therapies such as acupuncture, reflexology and Reiki as part of the programme.

Fees: (On application)

Primary Care: £1,512 a week
Secondary Care: £566 a week

Completion rates:
Primary Care: c80%
Secondary Care: c60%

• BROADREACH HOUSE

Location:
Plymouth, Devon.

Website:
www.broadreach-house.org.uk

Type of organisation:
Registered charity offering residential and day treatment services.

Services available to:
Both State-funded and private applicants.

Contact details for admission:
Residential:

Tel: 01752 797100
Email: enquiry@broadreach-house.org.uk

Postal address:
Broadreach
465 Tavistock Road
Plymouth
Devon
PL6 7HE

Day Service:

Tel: 01752 500003
Email: dayservice@broadreach-house.org.uk

Postal address:
Action for Change
Ocean Quay
Richmond Walk
Plymouth
PL1 4LL

Brief description of facilities/courses:

3 residential centres, 73 bed spaces, offering detox and rehabilitation for up to 6 months. Day services, including aftercare, resettlement, life-skills training and education/work opportunities. Parenting Programme and Supported Housing scheme also available.

Unusual features:

Doesn't use 12 Step approach, but motivational techniques such as cognitive behavioural therapy (CBT) and social learning interventions. Mixed and single sex residential units. Comprehensive service from detox through to resettlement. Day service very unusual in meeting complete range of needs under one roof.

Fees:

Residential: From £495 to £1,095 a week.
Day Care: £190 a week.

Completion rates:

Residential Programme: c65%
Day Programme: c80%

• ALCOHOL & DRUG ABSTINENCE SERVICE (ADAS)

Location:
Stockport, Cheshire.

Website:
www.adas.org.uk

Type of organisation:
Non-profit-making registered charity providing day care treatment (quasi-residential).

Services available to:
Those over 18 and motivated to complete abstinence. People can apply directly, and referrals are taken from GPs, the prison service and social services.

Contact details for admission:
Tel: 0161 484 0000
Fax: 0161 484 0011

Postal address:
ADAS
483 Buxton Road
Great Moor
Stockport
SK2 7HQ

Brief description of facilities/courses:
Structured day care treatment centre (quasi residential) supports males and females to become and remain abstinent from alcohol when they have completed a medical detox and are physically and mentally ready to change their thoughts and behaviours. The 12 Step abstinence programme, which consists of group work and one to one counselling, runs for 8 weeks and is followed by 12 week aftercare which runs 2 days per week. Acorn House provides beds for six males who attend the treatment centre and are homeless or live in an environment not conducive to treatment.

Costs:

Fees for the day care programme are £5,000. Costs for full treatment and accommodation are £8,000. Some charitable funds are available.

Success rate:

The programme has a 78% success rate.

• THE PRIORY HEALTHCARE GROUP

Location:
National chain with 14 hospitals.

Website:
www.prioryhealthcare.com

Type of organisation:
Independent provider of addiction treatment services.

Services available to:
Publicly, privately and self-funded patients, and all Priory hospitals are recognised by all major private medical insurers.

Contact details for admission:
Contact the admissions office of your nearest hospital, details of which can be obtained from the website or by phoning 0845 477 4679.

Brief description of facilities/courses:
Abstinence-based addiction treatment programme usually incorporates a 28+ day hospital stay supported by 12 months of structured aftercare. Treatment options range from a seven day inpatient detox for alcohol, to 48+ day interventions for more complex dual-diagnosis (addiction + another mental health issue). Also offers day patient and outpatient addiction treatment programmes and support and advice to family members.

Unusual features:
Provides an unusually large amount of individual treatment time – at any one time has 100 to 110 patients in addiction treatment programmes across 14 hospitals nationwide, helping over 1,200 people with addiction issues annually. The group offers anyone a free consultation with a trained addiction therapist.

Success rates:
According to a recent outcome study, up to 62% of Priory patients maintain total abstinence one year after discharge and enjoy significantly improved quality of life.

• KENWARD TRUST

Location:
Based in Yalding, near Maidstone, Kent.

Website:
www.kenwardtrust.org.uk

Type of organisation:
Registered Christian charity providing residential rehabilitation, day recovery projects, outreach services and local alcohol clinics.

Services available to:
State and privately-funded applicants; referrals taken from throughout the UK – funding essential.

Contact details for admission to rehab/daycare:
Tel: 01622 814187
Fax: 01622 815805
Email: enquiry@kenwardtrust.org.uk

On-line application:
Via website.

Postal address:
The Kenward Trust
Kenward House
Kenward Road
Yalding
Nr. Maidstone
Kent
ME18 6AH

Brief description of facilities/courses:
A total of 100 residential places (including 23 for young homeless men) and 160 places per year in structured day programmes. Cognitive/behavioural and 12 Step orientated therapy, detox, counselling, aftercare. Outreach services and local Alcohol Clinics in West Kent.

Unusual features:

As a Christian organisation, Kenward has success in re-establishing the infinite value of each individual (of all faiths and none), in contrast to the values and 'labels' placed on them by society at large.

Weekly fees:

Residential: c£500 per week depending on individual needs.
Structured Day Recovery (Maidstone and Tonbridge): Free to Kent residents and Kent Court referrals.

Completion rates:

Between 66% and 72% complete their programme and leave in a planned way.

• TURNING POINT

Location:
National organisation with nearly 250 service points across England and Wales.

Website:
www.turning-point.co.uk

Type of organisation:
A leading social care organisation, providing services for people with complex needs, including those affected by drug and alcohol misuse, mental health problems and those with a learning disability.

Services available to:
Varies depending on local need. Many services will accept referrals from any source, including GPs, other agencies and self-referrals. To search for Turning Point services and find out more about them and who they are available to, check www.turning-point.co.uk/Find+a+Service

Contact details for Head Office:
Standon House
21 Mansell St
London
E1 8AA
Tel: 020 7481 7600

Brief description of facilities/courses:
Turning Point's alcohol services include advice and education for young people, residential rehabilitation services, counselling, outreach work, and support services for friends and family members.

• ADDACTION

Location:
National.

Website:
www.addaction.org.uk

Type of organisation:
Drug and alcohol treatment charity, primary day care services but two residential rehab centres (Cornwall/SE London).

Services available to:
Alcohol applicants are primarily State-funded, although some for rehab are privately funded. Some family work is funded through charitable donations.

Contact details for admission:
Via your GP/social services.

Central office contact details:
Addaction Central Office
67-69 Cowcross Street
London
EC1M 6PU

Tel: 020 7251 5860
Fax: 020 7251 5890
Email: info@addaction.org

Brief description of facilities/courses:
Providing effective treatment through counselling and aftercare both for adults and, through its Youngaddaction services, for young people.

Unusual features:

Unusually large specialist alcohol and drug treatment agency. Now provides services to over 25,000 people a year in 70 services across the country. 9 services are dedicated to young people's services under the Youngaddaction brand.

• ACTION ON ADDICTION

Location:
National.

Website:
www.aona.co.uk

Type of organisation:
A registered charity which takes action to disarm addiction through research, residential and non-residential treatment, rehabilitation, dedicated support for families, prevention initiatives and professional education & training. Includes Clouds House residential rehab clinic (See Case Study, Chapter 3, page 42).

Services available to:
Anyone over 18, subject to assessment, and the availability of funding. Some financial support may be available.

Contact details:
Tel: 020 7793 1011
Fax: 020 7793 8549
Email: action@aona.co.uk

Postal address:
Action on Addiction
1st Floor
Park Place
12 Lawn Lane
London
SW18 1UD

Brief description of facilities:
A comprehensive service delivered by an expert multi-disciplinary team provides integrated medical and psychological treatment. Clouds House is a magnificent country house in a beautiful secluded location. Outpatient aftercare is available in Wiltshire and London. Specialist support for families.

Unusual features:

Benefits directly from the resources of Families Plus and The Centre for Addiction Treatment Studies, which teaches courses leading to degrees in Addiction Counselling awarded by the University of Bath.

Weekly costs:

Please enquire.

Completion/success rates:

Currently 83% complete detox and 72% complete treatment as a whole. An independent outcome evaluation indicated 61% of people were abstinent at a 30 month follow up.

• ADDICTION RECOVERY AGENCY (ARA)

Location:
Bristol.

Website:
www.addictionrecovery.org.uk

Type of organisation:
Registered charity providing treatment and support services for those with drink problems.

Services available to:
Those with drink problems, both locally and nationally. Most funding derived from local and national government sources.

Contact details:
Tel: 0117 930 0282
Fax: 0117 929 4810
Email: info@addictionrecovery.org.uk

Postal address:
ARA
King's Court
King Street
Bristol
BS1 4EE

Brief description of services offered:
A wide range of harm reduction and abstinence-based (12 Step) treatment and support services, including structured day care, residential rehabilitation, supported housing and aftercare.

Unusual features:
Offers the complete treatment journey, from initial information and advice to treatment and recovery.

Types of people most popular with:
Wide range, including families seeking support.

• CASTLE CRAIG HOSPITAL

Location:
West Linton, Scotland.

Website:
www. castlecraig.co.uk

Type of organisation:
Offers hospital inpatient treatment for those suffering from alcohol dependency and other addictions.

Services available to:
Both privately-funded and State-funded applicants.

Contact details for admission:
Tel: 01721 722763
Fax: 01721 752662
Email: enquiries@castlecraig.co.uk

Postal address:
Admissions Manager
Castle Craig Hospital
West Linton
Peeblesshire
Scotland
EH46 7DH

Brief description of facilities:

The main building houses up to 55 patients, and it is here that patients undergo detoxification for alcohol and then experience four to six weeks of intensive psychotherapy and, where necessary, help with existing mental and health problems. AA is very much part of the ethos and basis of therapy. A further 67 beds in the Extended Care Unit in the grounds enable patients to have extended care for anything up to six months. Throughout the campus there is 24 hour onsite medical cover by resident medical officers and nurses.

Unusual features:

Set in the Scottish Borders only 20 miles from Edinburgh and is contained within its own small estate of 50 acres. Additional therapies such as the exercise training programme in the gym and equine assisted therapy.

- ## ADFAM

Location:

London.

Website:

www.adfam.org.uk

Type of organisation:

National registered charity that supports families affected by drugs and alcohol.

Services available to:

Families nationally affected by drugs and alcohol.

Contact details:

Tel: 020 7553 7640

Fax: 020 7253 7991

Email: admin@adfam.org.uk

Postal Address:

Adfam

25 Corsham Street

London

N1 6DR

Brief description of services offered:

Provides an online database of local support groups and services for families, literature to help families better cope with the problems they face, training for families and professionals, and campaigning and lobbying to increase awareness of the problems families face and improve the resources available to them.

Unusual features:

Supports and campaigns on behalf of families affected by substance misuse.

Costs:

Funded through individual donations, charitable trusts and contracts for work undertaken. Accepts donations online.

Types of people most popular with:

Families of substance users and professionals that support the families of substance users.

- ## NATIONAL ASSOCIATION FOR CHILDREN OF ALCOHOLICS (NACOA)

Location:

Bristol, but provides national service.

Website:

www.nacoa.org.uk

Type of organisation:

Registered charity providing information, advice and support for children of alcohol-dependent parents and people concerned for their welfare.

Services available to:

Children and adult-children of alcohol-dependent parents and people concerned for their welfare.

Contact details:

Tel: 0117 924 8005
Fax: 0117 942 2928
Email: helpline@nacoa.org.uk

Postal Address:

NACOA
PO Box 64
Fishponds
Bristol
BS16 2UH

Brief description of services offered:

Telephone, email and letter helpline providing information, advice and support. The helpline service is provided for as long as the caller wishes to call. Website, information packs specific to individual callers, UK Resource database of services throughout the UK, volunteering and training programmes for volunteer helpline counsellors.

Unusual features:

Not 12 Step orientated, although has a good working relationship with Al-Anon. Provides information and advice on a range of subjects, some of which have only an indirect connection with alcoholism, i.e. self-harm, eating disorders, mental health problems. Work with callers as individuals, not simply extensions of parental alcoholism.

Costs:

None. Relies entirely on voluntary donations.

Types of people most popular with:

Children of alcohol-dependent parents.

3. ADDITIONAL SOURCES OF INFORMATION

- Additional residential rehab facilities in your area can be found from a national register on the National Treatment Agency for Substance Misuse's website:

www.nta.nhs.uk/about_treatment/treatment_directories/residential /resdirectory_f.aspx

- Details of 180 substance misuse services to help young people can also be obtained from a national register on the National Treatment Agency for Substance Misuse's website:

www.nta.nhs.uk/about_treatment/treatment_directories/young_pe ople

- Details of a wide range of counsellors and therapists can be obtained from The British Association for Counselling and Psychotherapy:

www.bacp.co.uk

4. STATE-FUNDED ORGANISATIONS

* Details of local drug and alcohol teams can be obtained from the Home Office website:

http://drugs.homeoffice.gov.uk/dat/directory

State-funded organisations mentioned in this book

* **KCA, ASHFORD** (See Case Study, Chapter 4, pages 85 to 87)

Website:
www.kca.org.uk

Contact details:
Tel: 01233 640040
Email: ashford@kca.org.uk
Postal address:
171 Beaver Road
Ashford
Kent
TN23 7SG

* **CROYDON COMMUNITY DRUG AND ALCOHOL CENTRE**
(See Case Study, Chapter 5, pages 106 to 107)

Contact details:
Tel: 020 3228 0200
Fax: 020 3228 0260/0261
Email: no general email but team leader email address can be obtained on website.
Postal address:
Croydon Substance Misuse Team
Ground floor, Crosfield house
Mint Walk
Croydon
CR9 3JS

5. SELF-HELP GROUPS

• ALCOHOLICS ANONYMOUS

National 12 Step orientated self-help group for those with drink problems (See Chapter 3, pages 42 to 43).

Website:
www.alcoholics-anonymous.org.uk

Website gives details of meetings nationwide and of local helpline numbers that can be used to confirm meetings. Do not use national helpline, which is for 12 Step use only, for confirming meetings.

National helpline:
0845 769 7555

Postal address for General Service Office:
The General Service Board of Alcoholics Anonymous (Great Britain) Limited
PO Box 1
10 Toft Green
York
YO1 7NJ

• AL-ANON FAMILY GROUPS

National self-help group for anyone whose life has been affected by other people's drinking (See Chapter 8, pages 162 to 164).

Website:
www.al-anonuk.org.uk

Contact details:
National helpline: 020 7403 0888
Fax: 020 7378 9910
Email: enquiries@al-anonuk.org.uk

Postal Address:
Al-Anon Family Groups UK & Eire
61 Great Dover Street
London
SE1 4YF

• ALATEEN

National self-help group for young people aged 12 to 17 affected by a problem drinker.

Contact details:
The same as for Al-Anon (see above).

- ## SMART RECOVERY UK

Location:

UK-wide.

Website:

www.smartrecovery.co.uk

Type of organisation:

Registered charity set up to support the development of a UK network of self-help groups, both face-to-face and web-based. Non-profit and volunteer-based organisation.

Services available to:

Those with alcohol problems who want to become abstinent or consider abstinence.

Contact details:

Telephone: 0845 603 9830

Fax: 01463 716003

Email: info@smartrecovery.co.uk

Postal address:

Fairways House
Fairways Business Park
Inverness
IV2 6AA

Brief description of services offered:

Provides free self-help groups and related services. Is evidence-based, teaches self-empowerment, and uses cognitive behavioural and motivational enhancement techniques to help participants achieve abstinence. Even those whose ultimate goal is moderation may benefit from participation in abstinence-oriented discussions.

Unusual Features:

SMART Recovery offers an alternative approach to the 12 Step model, and views addiction as a maladaptive behaviour rather than a disease. It is also adding a new Internet self-help approach for those who are not sure if they want to change.

Costs:

The meetings are free but donations are welcome

Types of people most popular with:

Those who do not like the 12 Step approach or who want practical and simple tools and techniques to help maintain recovery.

• MODERATION MANAGEMENT

Location:
New York, but online programmes accessible from UK.

Website:
www.moderation.org

Type of organisation:
International not-for-profit behavioural change programme and support group network for people concerned about their drinking and who desire to make positive lifestyle changes.

Services available to:
Any adult concerned about a drinking problem.

Contact details:
Tel: 001 212 871 0974
Email: mm@moderation.org
Fax: 001 212 213 6582

Postal address:
Moderation Management Network Inc.
C/o Harm Reduction Coalition,
5th Floor,
22 West 27th Street,
NY 10001
US

Brief description of services offered:
No face-to-face groups yet available in the UK but a professionally reviewed programme is available via the website. This provides information about alcohol, moderate drinking guidelines and limits, drink monitoring exercises, goal setting techniques and self-management strategies. Members also find balance and moderation in many other areas of their lives, one small step at a time.

Unusual features:

Helps with cutting down drinking as well as abstinence, depending on the informed preference of the individual. Offers an online personal drink tracking register and a chatroom (www.moderation.org/chat) for real-time communication between members, which generally replicates live face-to-face meetings.

Cost:

None. Entirely supported by donations.

Types of people most popular with:

Around two thirds of users are women.

• SOS INTERNATIONAL

Location:

Hollywood, US (but has UK presence).

Website:

www.sossobriety.org

Type of organisation:

SOS (Secular Organisations for Sobriety/Save Our Selves) offers an abstinence-based alternative self-help group to AA. Non-profit organisation.

Services available to:

Those with drink problems.

Contact details:

Details of UK meetings should be obtained via the US operation.

Tel: 001 323 666 4295

Email: SOS@CFIWest.org

Postal address:

Save Our Selves (SOS)
4773 Hollywood Blvd
Hollywood
CA 90027
US

Brief description of services offered:

Provides self-empowerment support group meetings. Each meeting is autonomous and held on an anonymous basis at no charge to participants.

Unusual features:

Differs from AA in not taking 12 Step based spiritual approach.

Types of people most popular with:

Those seeking an alternative to AA's spiritual approach.

• CO-DEPENDENTS ANONYMOUS (CoDA)

Location:
National.

Website:
www.coda-uk.org

Type of organisation:
Not–for-profit self-help group for those self-identifying as co-dependents. 12 Step orientated, not a registered charity.

Services available to:

Adults experiencing relationship difficulties, seeking healthy and fulfilling relationships with themselves and others. Co-dependent relationship patterns often involve seeking to control another person's behaviour, being unaware or denying one's own needs and inwardly feeling confusion, fear or shame.

Contact details:
Initial enquirers phone the local group contact, or just turn up (see website).
Email: coda-uk@hotmail.com

Postal address:
PO Box 2365
Bristol
BS6 9XJ

Brief description of services offered:
Members' experience is that regular attendance at meetings and actively following the programme's suggestions leads in time to radically improved relationships and inner peace.

Meetings follow a set pattern, designed to make efficient use of time, and welcome and encourage those present. All personal information is treated in the strictest confidence and bureaucracy is minimal.

Unusual features:

Far cheaper, more anonymous and more flexible than most conventional therapies.

Cost:

Group expenses, including the cost of the meeting, are covered by donations from members. Donations from non-members are not accepted.

6. ALTERNATIVE MEDICINE

Details of practitioners for acupuncture, counselling, healing, homeopathy, reflexology, Reiki, Indian Head Massage and nutrition can be obtained from:

- ## THE BRITISH COMPLEMENTARY MEDICINE ASSOCIATION

Website:
www.bcma.co.uk

Contact details:
Tel: 0845 345 5977

Postal address:
BCMA
P.O. Box 5122
Bournemouth
BH8 0WG

• BANYAN RETREAT

Location:
Hothfield, near Ashford, Kent.

Website:
www.banyanretreat.com

Type of organisation:
Natural Healing centre (see Chapter 3).

Available to:
Private applicants.

Contact details:
Tel: 01233 714155
Email: info@banyanretreat.com

Postal address:
Banyan Retreat
Lake House
Maidstone Road
Hothfield
Ashford
Kent
TN26 1AR

Brief description of treatment/courses relevant to overcoming alcohol problems:
Nutritionists – although they do not actually offer a cure, various supplements may help overcome the craving for alcohol and give support during the withdrawal process. Obviously, nutritional supplements are safer than prescription drugs which may have unpleasant side effects.

Reflexology – helps in detoxification and relaxing the body, reduces tension and induces a calmer and more relaxed frame of mind.

Indian Head Massage, meditation and Reiki – helps to relax the body, reduce tension and induce a calmer and more relaxed frame of mind.

Meditation – helps to relax the body, reduce tension and induce a calmer and more relaxed frame of mind.

Reiki – helps to relax the body, reduce tension and induce a calmer and more relaxed frame of mind.

Unusual features:
   Calming and peaceful environment.

Fees:
   Nutritional Support – £50 initial one hour consultation.
   Reflexology – £28
   Indian Head Massage – £25
   Meditation – £5
   Reiki – No charge with other treatment.

- ## THE HALE CLINIC

Location:

Central London, W1

Website:

www.haleclinic.com

Type of organisation:

Health centre (See Chapters 2, 3 and 4).

Available to:

Private and State-funded applicants. A charity to help fund treatment could be established in 2008.

Contact details for admission for treatment:

Tel: 020 7631 0156

Fax: 020 7580 5771

Email: admin@haleclinic.com

Postal Address:

The Hale Clinic

7 Park Crescent

London

W1B 1PF

Brief description of treatment relevant to beating alcohol problems:

Nutrition, EEG Neurofeedback, Acupuncture, Colonic Irrigation, Hypnotherapy, Energy Alignment, Spiritual Healing, Reiki Reflexology, Indian Head Massage, Meditation. Some of these treatments can be used as one of the main treatment modalities for alcoholism while others will take a more supportive, nurturing role.

Unusual features:

Uses an integrated team approach which will use nutrition, psychology, energy medicine and healing. Does not see one modality having the whole answer to solving addiction. It is a multi-faceted approach. Also looks at creating a new life, new friends for those recovering from drink problems so that their environment does not pull them back into their old habits. It can even send practitioners to patients' homes during recovery to help them structure a new life. Advisory service which will help patients work out the most appropriate treatment programme for them.

- ## DR. SURINDER KAUR

  Director of EEG Neurofeedback (See Chapter 4, pages 78-80). Uses innovative techniques involving specialist video games and claims a success rate of around 95%. Works at Hale Clinic (see contact details on page 261), and at EEG Neurofeedback Services, St. Albans.

Website:
  www.eegneurofeedback.net

Contact details:
  (St. Albans)
  Tel/Fax: 01727 874 292
  Email: drkaur@eegneurofeedback.net

Postal address:
  PO Box 895
  St Albans
  AL1 9EH

• DIRK BUDKA

Nutritionist, Microbiologist and Allergologist (See Chapter 3, page 47).

Websites:
www.nutritionlondon.net
www.ibsforum.co.uk
www.parasiteclinic.com
www.stop-readymeals.com

Contact details:
Tel: 020 7704 6900

Dirk Budka works at:
Healthy Living Centre
282-284 St Paul's Road
London
N1 2LH

Website: www.thehealthylivingcentre.co.uk

The Hale Clinic: See page 261 for contact details

Neal's Yard Therapy Rooms

Contact details:
Tel: 020 7379 7662
Email: therapyrooms@nealsyardremedies.com

Postal address:
2 Neal's Yard
Covent Garden
London
WC2H 9DP

Contact details:
   Tel: 020 7223 7141
   Email: clapham@nealsyardremedies.com

Postal address:
     Neal's Yard Therapy Rooms
     6 Northcote Road
     Clapham
     London
     SW11 1NT

Contact details:
   Tel: 020 7940 1414
   Email: boroughmarket@nealsyardremedies.com

Postal address:
     Neal's Yard Remedies
     4 Bedale Street
     Borough Market
     London
     SE1 9AL

7. HYPNOTHERAPY

Details of hynotherapists can be obtained from The Hypnotherapy Association:

Website:
www.thehypnotherapyassociation.co.uk

Contact details:
Tel/Fax: 01257 262 124
Email: theha@tiscali.co.uk

Postal address:
The Hypnotherapy Association
14 Crown Street
Chorley
Lancashire
PR7 1DX

• RICK MACZKA (See Chapter 5)

Website:
www.rickmaczka.com

Contact details:
Tel: 01603 666546
Mobile: 07787 542765
Email: rick.maczka@btinternet.com

Postal address:
Complementary Health Care Clinic
34 Exchange Street
Norwich
NR2 1AX

- **PAULINE HAVELOCK-SEARLE,**
  Hypnotherapist/Hypnoanalyst (who cured Edmund
  Tirbutt – See Chapter 3)

Website:

    www.paulinehavelockhypnotherapy.co.uk

Contact details:

    Tel: 020 8723 5840
    Mobile: 07956 154 887
    Email: pauline.havelock@ntlworld.com

8. SPIRITUAL HEALING

Details of spiritual healers can be obtained from The National Federation of Spiritual Healers:

Website:
www.nfsh.org.uk

Contact details:
Tel: 0845 1232777
Fax: 01932 779648
Email: office@nfsh.org.uk

Postal address:
NFSH
Old Manor Farm Studio
Church Street
Sunbury-on-Thames
Middlesex
TW16 6RG

- **DAVID CUNNINGHAM (See Chapter 5)**

Website:
www.spiritualhealingcentre.com

Contact details:
Tel: 0191 417 8231
Mobile: 07903 627433

9. THE WORKPLACE

• EMPLOYEE ASSISTANCE PROGRAMMES (EAPs)

Details of EAP providers can be obtained from the Employee Assistance Professionals Association (EAPA):

Website:
www.eapa.org.uk

Contact details:
Tel: 0800 783 7616
Fax: 01993 772765
Email: info@eapa.org.uk

Postal address:
UK Employee Assistance Professionals Association
3 Moors Close
Ducklington
Witney
Oxfordshire
OX29 7TW

• AXA PPP HEALTHCARE EAP SERVICES (See Chapter 9)

Website:
www.axappphealthcare.co.uk

Contact details:
Tel: 0800 170 800

Postal address:
AXA PPP healthcare
Employee Support
Phillips House
Tunbridge Wells
Kent
TN1 2PL

• OCCUPATIONAL HEALTH SERVICES

Details of providers of occupational health can be obtained from the Commercial Occupational Health Providers Association (COHPA):

Website:
www.cohpa.co.uk

Contact details:
Tel: 01933 303007
Fax: 01933 303001
Email: info@cohpa.co.uk

Postal address:
COHPA
Wellingborough Innovation Centre
Church Street
Wellingborough
Northamptonshire
NN8 4PD

- ## BUPA OCCUPATIONAL HEALTH Ltd (See Chapter 9)

Website:

www.bupa.co.uk/wellness/asp/corporate/services_overview/occ
upational_health

Contact details:

Tel: 0845 606 6736
Fax: 0161 254 3643
Email: drug&alc@bupa.com

Postal address:

BUPA Occupational Health Ltd
3rd Floor, Victoria Building
Harbour City
Quays Loop Rd
Salford
Manchester
M50 3SP

- ## BUSINESS PSYCHOLOGISTS

  Details of business psychologists can be obtained from the Association of Business Psychologists:

  Website:
  www.theabp.org

- ## KATE KEENAN, CHARTERED OCCUPATIONAL PSYCHOLOGIST (See Chapter 9)

  Website:
  www.keenan-research.com

  Contact details:
  Tel: 01225 336569
  Email: kmkeenan@keenan-research.com

  Postal address:
  Keenan Research Ltd, Business Psychology, Coaching & Consultancy
  Victoria House
  15 Gay Street
  Bath
  BA1 2PH

- **DR. JOAN HARVEY, CHARTERED PSYCHOLOGIST (See Chapter 9)**

Website:
www.ncl.ac.uk/psychology/staff/profile/joan.harvey

Contact details:
Tel: 0191 222 8829
Email: joan.harvey@ncl.ac.uk

Postal address:
Dr. Joan Harvey
School of Psychology
Newcastle University
Newcastle upon Tyne
NE1 7RU

10. SELLERS OF DE-ALCOHOLISED DRINKS

• THE ALCOHOL-FREE SHOP

Location:
Manchester, but provides national delivery service.

Website:
www.alcoholfree.co.uk

Type of organisation:
Seller of de-alcoholised wines, beers and other products.

Contact details:
Tel: 0845 388 3068
Fax: 0845 388 3069
Email: info@alcoholfree.co.uk

Postal Address:
The Alcohol-Free Shop
202-208 Cheetham Hill Road
Manchester
M8 8LW

Brief description of de-alcoholised produce offered:
A range of alcohol-free and de-alcoholised wine (including organics), beers, spirits, liqueurs, and soft drinks plus alcohol-free toiletries, beauty products including Halal certificated, cold remedies, health supplements and confectionery.

Unusual features:
Caters for people who avoid alcohol for any reason from those adopting sensible drinking habits to recovering alcoholics or those, such as Muslims, observing strict religious rules on abstinence. Its range includes Halal products. Its website provides well-researched, professionally written information about alcohol and it offers a small selection of books for further reading.

Costs:

(Examples)

Wines from £2.99 to £6.85, sparkling wines from £4.99 to £7.99, beers from £16.49 to £19.99 for 24 bottles/cans. Free delivery on some products.

Types of consumers most popular with:

Individuals who want to cut down on or abstain from alcohol, event organisers and restaurants.

• THE LONO DRINKS COMPANY

Location:
Gloucestershire, but provides national delivery service.

Website:
www.lono.co.uk

Type of organisation:
Mail order alcohol-free drinks specialist.

Contact details:
Tel: 01285 850682
Fax: 01285 850455
Email: info@lono.co.uk

Postal Address:
The Hawthorns
Driffield
Cirencester
Gloucestershire
GL7 5PY

Brief description of de-alcoholised produce offered:
Over 50 alcohol-free and de-alcoholised wines, aperitifs, spirits, beer and cider, from all over the world.

Unusual features:
Prides itself on personal service and on offering the widest available choice. It was the pioneer in safe drinking and its portfolio was the world's first. There is an open advisory telephone line to help newcomers choose their best product options.

Costs:
Wines are a modest £3.40 for a choice of German and French white, rosé, or red, to £7.50 for the world-class Californian range. Organic wines vary from £5.49 to £6.85. Bubbly's start at £3.99 with the popular Carl Jung Brut at only £4.99. Spirits and aperitifs start at £4.50 for an apple schnapps and whisky at £4.90. Cocktails, such as kiwi/lime (Margherita), are £4.75.

Types of consumers most popular with:

Expectant mothers, middle-aged to seniors, females in late 20s/early 30s, drivers and pilots, slimmers, wedding parties, corporate entertainment, athletes, religious groups, stage and entertainment world.

11. OTHER USEFUL WEBSITES AND HELPLINES

Free confidential advice on drinking problems can be obtained from:

- **NHS Direct:** 0845 4647

- **FRANK:**   0800 776600

- **Drinkline:**   0800 917 8282

- **ChildLine:** (For youngsters) 0800 1111

- **The Samaritans:** (Provides someone to listen if you are in crisis, despair and suicidal)
  Website: www.samaritans.org.uk
  Tel: 08457 909090

Other useful information sources:

- **Alcohol Concern:** (Useful information)
  Website: www.downyourdrink.org.uk

- **The Drinkaware Trust** (Information on responsible drinking)
  Website: www.drinkawaretrust.co.uk

- **Think About Drink** (Useful information from the NHS)
  Website: www.wrecked.co.uk

Other people/organisations mentioned in this book

- **Joe Simpson** (See Chapter 1, page 16)
  Website: www.noordinaryjoe.co.uk

- **The British Liver Trust**
  Website: www.britishlivertrust.org.uk
  Tel: 0870 770 8028

- **The Health & Safety Executive**
  Website: www.hse.gov.uk
  Tel: 0845 3450055

- **DVLA**
  Website: www.dvla.gov.uk (Lists local offices)

- **Unum**
  Website: www.unum.co.uk
  Tel: 01306 887766

- **AEGON Scottish Equitable**
  Website: www.aegonse.co.uk
  Tel: 0845 600 1402

Index

A

L

Lifestyle changes 92, 110

Liver

    Damage – symptoms 46, 205

    Disease 203

    How the liver processes alcohol 25

LoNo Drinks Company 87, 88-89, 276-277

M

Maczka, Rick 117-118

McGrath, Patrick 181-182

McHugh, Kate 169, 190, 192

McPhillips, Dr. Mike 39, 59, 104

Medical detox 12-14

Medical records 45, 53, 100-106, 109,

Meditation vii, 49, 55, 118, 260-161

Memory loss 11, 12, 38, 124-125, 151, 160-161

Mental illness 24, 65, 95, 188, 128, 218,

Middleton, Dr. Scott 170, 195-196

Moderation Management 78, 253-254

Muslim (*See* Islam)

N

National Association for Children of Alcoholics, The 164, 245-246

National Federation of Spiritual Healers, The 119, 268

National Treatment Agency 148, 215, 218, 247

NHS Direct 11, 278

Non-alcoholic wines and beers 50, 88- 89

Nutrition 46-47

O

Occupational Health providers 183, 187, 270-271

O'Donnell, Prof. Michael 45, 180, 192, 194

Outpatient treatment 234, 239

Y